First, a few words
from people whose animals are featured in the book

Some people think their pets are just animals. If you are one of these people, you are probably not reading this book. Learning animal communication has not only shown me how to help other people understand their animals, but it has taught me how to pay attention! Babette's book and participation in my learning process have broadened my perspective on sharing this planet with my own animals and all animals I encounter.

~Celia Lambert

I first contacted Babette to find out why my puppy Tango ate his own poop and woke me up in the middle of the night. He let her know that apparently poo tastes "tangy," and after his conversation with her, he resisted the urge to eat it so he could continue to get puppy kisses. The explanation of his nighttime ramblings contained information that Babette could not have known from any source other than Tango himself. Six months later, I took Babette's animal communication class, and I continue to use those skills every day to enhance the enjoyment of life for all of us in the pack.

~Jenn Reed

I'm very thankful I found Babette when I did. I wished I had come to her 2 years sooner. She helped me understand why my cat Sweetie Pie was fighting with Boots so much. Babette was instrumental in resolving years' long issues between my cats. I enjoyed this book immensely!

~Kevin Wattier

In addition to her help with my dog Clover, whose story is in this book, Babette also helped me with my dog Brownie, who had a large tumor behind his eye. Through her communication with him we learned that what I assumed was thunder storm phobia was actually distress caused by the change in barometric pressure, most likely affecting the tumor. This insight helped me to make his last few months more comfortable. The workshops I've attended with Babette have enabled me to develop my own ability to communicate with critters. I do believe that we all have the potential to do this, and her book is a great way to get started.

~Lauren Thomas

I am in awe of Babette's work and dedication. She has helped all six of my animals, each of whom had problems that were resolved by her communication and healing. Her ability to communicate with animals and translate so their humans can understand has inspired me to learn animal communication for myself. I'm still learning, and I know that with the tools she has provided and my continued practice, over time I can gain the ability to become as adept as she is at animal communication.

~Daike Klement

When Babette came to Panther Ridge, I witnessed a relationship that I thought was unattainable. Babette and Macho the ocelot were locked in each other's gaze, communicating on a level that I can only strive for... kindred spirits exchanging information unknowable to the average person. Babette was able to bring his former suffering into perspective that gave me even more respect for my incredible ocelot and for Babette's unique sensitivity. If you have ever wanted a deeper understanding of the animals in your life, dive into "Hear Them Speak" and believe in your ability.

~Judy Berens
Panther Ridge Conservation Center

Hear Them Speak

Hear Them Speak

A Twelve-Week Course in
Telepathic Animal Communication

Babette de Jongh

READ, RESCUE, REPEAT
Reno, NV

Hear Them Speak

A Twelve-Week Course in Telepathic Animal Communication

Copyright ©2019 by Babette de Jongh

All rights reserved. This book or portions thereof may not be reproduced, stored, or transmitted in any form or by any means without written permission from the publisher, except by a reviewer, who may quote brief passages in a review.

Edited by Brass Ring Edits
Cover design by The Killion Group
Cover photograph by Andrea McDaniel

The material in this book is intended for education. No expressed or implied guarantee as to the effects of the use of the recommendations can be given nor liability taken. Please use common sense and stay safe when interacting with animals.

Library of Congress Control Number: 2019934674

```
Publisher's Cataloging-In-Publication Data
(Prepared by The Donohue Group, Inc.)

Names: De Jongh, Babette, author.
Title: Hear them speak : a twelve-week course in telepathic animal
   communication / Babette de Jongh.
Description: Reno, NV : Dogs & Books, [2019]
Identifiers: ISBN 9780999843024 (paperback) | ISBN 0999843028
   (paperback) | ISBN 9780999843031 (ebook) | ISBN 0999843036 (ebook)
Subjects: LCSH: Human-animal communication--Handbooks, manuals, etc. |
   Extrasensory perception in animals--Handbooks, manuals, etc. |
   Telepathy--Handbooks, manuals, etc.
Classification: LCC QL776 .D4 2019 (print) | LCC QL776 (ebook) | DDC
   591.59--dc23
```

Babette de Jongh

This book is dedicated to all the animals who taught me how to hear them speak, most especially to Jack Skellington de Jongh, the three-legged Best Good Dog who blasted into our lives and burrowed into our hearts, where he will live forevermore.

We will miss you, Mr. Jack, until you decide to come back again.

Table of Contents

Foreword by Jack Rudloe i
Author's Note vii
Acknowledgments ix
Introduction 1
LESSON ONE: Thinking Back 5
    Highlights 15
    Tasks 16
LESSON TWO: Laying the Foundation 19
    Highlights 46
    Tasks 47
LESSON THREE: Getting Started 49
    Highlights 69
    Tasks 71
LESSON FOUR: Visual Information 73
    Highlights 87
    Tasks 89
LESSON FIVE: Auditory Information 91
    Highlights 106
    Tasks 108
LESSON SIX: Feeling Information 111
    Highlights 136
    Tasks 138
LESSON SEVEN: Smell, Taste, and Knowing 141
    Highlights 157

Tasks	158
LESSON EIGHT: Common Blocks, Digging Deeper	161
Highlights	196
Tasks	197
LESSON NINE: Troubleshooting	199
Highlights	225
Tasks	227
LESSON TEN: Communicating with Clients and Counseling Multispecies Families	229
Highlights	248
Tasks	250
LESSON ELEVEN: Special Challenges	251
Highlights	286
Tasks	287
LESSON TWELVE: Own Your Superpowers	289
Highlights	317
Tasks	318
Appendix One: More about Meditation	320
Appendix Two: Psychic and Emotional Protection	334
Appendix Three: Index of Figures	337
Appendix Four: Resources	350

Foreword

By Jack Rudloe

Animals communicate with us all the time. My cat yowls at me when he wants to be fed. My dogs give me the usual "feed me" or "take me for a walk" messages by wagging their tails and imploring me with big sad eyes. My son's rat terrier Shark Bait says, *Woof, woof, woof,* incessantly which, in the context of the park, means "Ball, ball... ball. Throw the ball!" No need for deep psychic understanding there.

But some animals are more mysterious. Like octopuses.

Gulf Specimen Marine Lab in Panacea, Florida, has all the usual sharks, sea turtles, sea horses and creatures that most aquariums have, but above all people are fascinated with our octopuses.

These eight-armed creatures with multiple brains will leave their rocky lair, jet across the tank, and "hold hands" with a visitor, wrapping its tentacles with their thousands of sucker disks around their hand. It's a scary experience because you think they might bite, which they almost never do. Then when they're finished exploring you, you're dismissed. They abruptly let go and swim off, leaving you to feel as though you've just been touched by an alien creature that is different from all other life forms on earth.

A friend of mine spent hours communicating with one and developing what she thought was a rapport. When it dropped her abruptly, she was left emotionally drained, lamenting that she was "kicked to the curb by an octopus."

On one memorable school field trip, an obnoxious young boy declared that the octopus was ugly and disgusting, and he instantly got squirted in the face, bringing much laughter from his classmates.

Octopus\human interactions have always been one of my interests, and over the past fifty years since I began Gulf Specimen Marine Lab in Panacea, Florida, visiting scientists have come from around the world to study octopus behavior.

They do all the classical experiments like putting a crab in a glass jar and watching the octopus unscrew the lid to extract it. One researcher played music to them, and determined that they respond best to the middle "c" notes.

World attention was drawn when "Paul the Octopus," sitting in an aquarium at a Germany bar, accurately predicted that Germany would win over Spain in the 2008 World Cup games. To see if our "Panacea Paula" octopus could predict the winner of the 2015 Super Bowl, we used the same methodology. We placed the logos of the Seattle Seahawks and the New England Patriots on two clear choice boxes, then put a crab in each--and waited. The unfortunate crab in the Patriot's Box got snatched first, and the Patriots defeated the Seahawks 28 to 24. So maybe they could win the lottery for us...

We lined up numbered pool balls in their tank. When they played with the balls and dragged them off to their burrows, we played the chosen numbers, and they won! Only they picked winning numbers a day late, and I got the feeling that they were playing me. Hence when I met Babette de Jongh at a book signing event in Apalachicola and learned that she is a professional animal communicator, I couldn't wait to see what she could do with our octopuses. Just by looking at a photograph, Babette uses mental telepathy and melds her mind with an animal. She learns why the dog bites, why the cat insists in pooping in the flower pot, or why someone's pet parrot suddenly stops eating. She learns her subject's fears, anxieties, and health problems, takes dictation and relates their problems to the animal's human in reports written the King's English, and suggests strategies, often involving energy healing, to fix the problem.

When I told my adult son about her work, and how she communicates with animals through mental telepathy, he thought it hysterical. I'd added another crackpot to my collection of weird people, like the Mississippi photographer who insisted that he was abducted by aliens, or the archeologist who divined buried prehistoric native artifacts by simply walking through the woods, stopping, pointing to the ground and demanding that his students dig there. (And when they did, they found thousand-year-old Native American artifacts.) Of course, there's also the highly credible embryologist from Canada who volunteers at our aquarium. She sees ghosts and got into an argument with one who insisted in standing in her parking spot at our dock facilities. When my wife passed away in 2012, Natalie Gordon connected with her spirit and relayed information to me that she could never have known about otherwise; hence I had proof of an afterlife.

So when Babette de Jongh came to Panacea, I needed proof that animal communication was real—and I got it. I asked her if she could do anything with Shark Bait, my son's ten-year-old rat terrier that had developed a sudden terror of flies. Whenever one got into the house, he panicked, hid in the closet for hours and sometimes days, refusing to come out. Holding him in her lap, Babette did a mind meld with him, but shook her head saying, "All I can get out of him is a rant, 'I hate flies' again and again." Until he finally told her how a yellow jacket stung him in the mouth, causing agonizing pain. My son was astounded; there was no way Babette could know that a few weeks ago, when his family was up in Georgia, Shark Bait snapped at a yellow fly, was stung in the mouth, went into hysterics, and had to be taken to the vet for a shot to calm him down.

So, onto the octopuses.

I led Babette into the Mother Ocean room of our aquarium and introduced her to our octopuses. But this particular batch, having just arrived, were adjusting to captivity and weren't particularly receptive.

But after Babette put her hand in the tank and focused on one, it left its grotto, came over, and wrapped its tentacles around her fingers. They "held hands" until the octopus tried to pull her into the tank. As she relates in this book, when she told the octopus that she wasn't willing to be dragged in, it let go and swam off, leaving her with a feeling of disappointment and rejection. She turned to me and said in amazement, "I've never experienced anything like this before. I feel that I've just been downloaded. It's like they're from another planet, another universe."

Octopuses may be from outer space. Certainly, their genome is different than any other animal on earth. So when the day comes that science fiction movies come true and spaceships arrive on earth, let us hope that animal communicators will be there ahead of the military and scientists to greet them.

If enough people read this book and complete the twelve-week course, the world could be a far better place. If we could communicate with other species, we might stop destroying their habitats and exterminating endangered species. We might realize that they have bodies, minds and spirits which are similar to ours.

And perhaps if we were kinder to them, we might be kinder to ourselves.

--Jack Rudloe, president of Gulf Specimen Marine Laboratories, Inc., and author of the *Erotic Ocean*, *The Living Dock*, *Time of the Turtle* and other books.

April 27, 2019

Author's Note

This book is not intended to convince anyone of anything. People who don't believe that telepathic animal communication exists will not find proof here. For proof-seekers, studies are available online, so I won't waste your time (or mine) repeating available information. Any proof that you receive will come from your personal experiences with your animal teachers.

Learning to communicate with animals, heart to heart and mind to mind, is the point and promise of this book. Hard hearts and closed minds need not apply, and your degree of success will be commensurate with your willingness to learn and practice. But you won't be going it alone; when it's time to start practicing, you'll be invited to join an online forum of fellow students with whom you can share the journey.

The easy-to-follow course is supported by relevant real-life examples that give context to the lessons. In most cases, I received permission from my human clients to use their animal companions' names, stories, and photographs. However, during in-person readings at public events, I often come away without every participant's contact info. In those cases, I changed the names, descriptions, and identifying details of those involved. I also did this when the ghost of a deceased neighbor haunted a family and their dog. Though the dog's family would have been happy to give permission for me to use their story, the neighbor's family had moved away, and even if they hadn't, out of respect for their loss, I wouldn't have asked.

Other stories, such as the true-to-life but fictional character of Rex, are amalgamations of separate encounters. It's a completely made-up tale that illustrates how an animal's experiences can shape their personalities.

If you'll let it, this book will guide you through every step toward developing your ability to Hear Them Speak. If you have questions or want to share successes and figure out failures, your fellow students and I will be there to help. I look forward to meeting you in the online forum soon!

Acknowledgments

I had plenty of assistance in bringing this book from idea to finished product. But even before the idea, I had to learn to accept and embrace my abilities, and for that, I have to thank the hundreds (or thousands? I don't do math) of animals who invited me into their minds and hearts.

Thanks to Jack Rudloe, president of Gulf Coast Marine Laboratories, for taking the time to read the book and write the foreword, and for encouraging me to tell the octopus story.

Thanks to my friend Licia Berry for her intuitive coaching and encouragement, and for her sage advice that gave me the focus I needed when multiple projects demanded my attention. Licia's words "You MUST write this book before you do *anything* else!" had enormous power to light a fire under me.

Thanks to Penelope Smith for her accessibility and mentorship, and for graciously giving me permission to include her insightful questions that will help the people who are reading this book initiate meaningful conversations with animals.

Thanks to my fellow animal communicators and friends, Anne-Laure Michelis, Therese Clinton, Griffin Kanter, Nefesh Chaya, Stacy Krafczyk, and Rachael Millikan, for their support and encouragement, and for sharing part of their journeys with me.

I also appreciate every animal communicator who shared their insight and wisdom through the books they wrote, the classes they taught, and the examples they set for our growing tribe. If not for those of you who shared your stories with the world, I would never have understood that my experiences were true animal communication and not just my imagination. Thank you for passing the torch to me. I'll keep it safe and pass it on.

Thank you to my students for helping me to learn even more by teaching them. Special thanks to one student in particular, Christine Althaea Abbey, for reading the first few chapters and providing feedback that helped me hone the message.

Thanks to Brass Ring Edits for keeping me (and my margins) straight, and to the generous beta-readers who offered to read and review the Advance Reader Copy. Special thanks to beta reader Cheryl Giebel for going through the ARC with a fine-toothed comb.

Thanks to everyone who generously provided photographs and artwork, and to those who allowed me to tell their animals' stories. Without you, this book would not exist.

Thanks to my kids, Christopher, Tessa, and Natalie, for being exactly who you are, and to my husband, Hans, for everything.

Finally, thanks to you, the reader, for taking the time to read this book and devote your time and energy to completing the course. I hope you will join the tribe of animal communicators who really do have the power to save the world, one happy ending at a time.

Introduction

Hear Them Speak

A Twelve-Week Course in
Telepathic Animal Communication

Figure 1: *You've already communicated telepathically with animals many times. But until you learn the difference between receiving true communication and creating something in your imagination, you won't know whether you're communicating or not. Soon, you'll have the tools to enter the space of communication at will. Animals will be your best teachers! Here are two of mine, L-R: Mr. Jack, The Best Good Dog, and Princess Julie-Jules, a Diva who likes to roll in dead things.*

I hope you're excited, because you're about to claim and understand how to use the power of telepathic animal communication you were born with. You already know how to do this, and in fact, you've been doing it all your life. All you need is for someone to validate what you've been seeing and hearing and knowing, and teach you how to recognize and harness that skill.

Many professional animal communicators (including me) have been communicating with animals since childhood, but didn't understand what was happening until much later in life. This book will help you unearth any buried memories of communication and shine a light on moments of communication that were mislabeled in your mind as something else.

The way this book is set up, you'll hit the ground running. Every lesson will begin with a dose of theory supported by plenty of anecdotes and pictures, and end with a set of tasks to do. I recommend that you spend a week on each lesson. Read the weekly lesson on day one of each week, and spend the rest of the week doing the assigned tasks, which by week three will include practicing your communication skills with one animal helper each day. I believe that your commitment to completing the twelve-week course in this way will yield results far beyond your expectations.

You can, of course, take as long as you like to read the book; and whether you decide to practice or complete any of the tasks is up to you. If you intend this book to be nothing more than interesting bedside reading, you'll still gain theoretical knowledge

Introduction

that will probably increase your abilities. However, I hope that you will use this book as a guide, follow the program as it was intended, and allow me to mentor you on the journey to becoming a competent telepathic animal communicator. Whether or not you give this course your time and attention for the duration of the twelve week course, you are likely to receive in direct proportion to what you give.

In the first lesson, I'll tell my story to give you an idea of what childhood animal communication looks like and how it evolves over a lifetime. You may even recognize your own experiences in my story. Lesson two will cover some basic tools that will help you access your intuition. In lesson three, we'll explore the theory behind telepathic communication, including what each mode of reception (seeing, hearing, feeling, tasting, smelling, and knowing) feels like, so you'll begin to recognize communication when it happens. That's the foundation we'll build on.

While you're practicing and learning, subsequent lessons will explore each mode of reception more deeply, adding detail and making that foundation more weighty and solid as we go.

By the midpoint of the course, we'll be troubleshooting what's getting in your way when you're not sure whether what you're getting is real or imagined. You'll recognize when you're blocking yourself, and blast through those blocks. You'll recognize when someone else is blocking you, and blast through those blocks, too.

You will learn about practical ways that communication can help animals, their human companions, and the world. You'll also learn about some of the metaphysical and spiritual concerns you may encounter while doing this work.

At the end of the course, you'll learn to use your newfound superpowers in a responsible and ethical way that will enhance your own life and make the world a better place. And, if you want to take your skills to the next level and offer your telepathic abilities to paying clients, you'll learn how to set up a professional animal communication business that you can be proud of.

So, are you ready? Let's dig in!

LESSON ONE: Thinking Back

In this lesson, I'll tell you about my first animal communication experiences, and you'll begin to uncover yours, even those you may have forgotten or dismissed.

***Figure* 2:** *In the old, grainy photos that remain of me as a child, it seemed I was almost-always holding a dog or a cat. In this photo: a Pekingese puppy.*

I've been communicating with animals all my life, but I didn't realize that's what was happening until I was in my late 30s. I can hear you asking, "How can you *not* know you're communicating with animals?" I thought the same thing myself when I read about people who claimed they were telepathic or psychic or whatever all their lives, but didn't know it until later.

I mean, how can you *not* know when animals are communicating with you, and you with them? Wouldn't that take a special kind of stupid?

Not really. Most people have probably communicated with animals without knowing it was happening. Hang on; I'll explain. Let me start by going back.

When I was a kid, I was very interested in and connected to animals. I liked animals. I wanted to touch them, hold them, spend time with them. I noticed them, often when other people didn't. It seemed that I was an animal magnet, always bringing home strays—cats, dogs, birds, even a baby skunk and a baby raccoon. So in that regard, I probably *was* a little bit special. If you weren't—or aren't—an animal magnet, that's okay; it doesn't mean you won't be good at communicating. It just means your floors will be cleaner than mine because your house won't be full of animals coming in and going out.

When I was about five years old, I found a baby skunk who'd been cornered by some barking dogs. I chased the dogs away and ran to get my daddy, who knew how to pick up the baby skunk, tucking its tail under so it couldn't "spray." The skunk lived with us—in an outdoor hutch—until he reached maturity. Then my daddy took him into the woods near our house and let him go. But Daddy didn't tell me that. He told me that my beloved skunk had escaped his cage and gone into the woods "to be free."

I knew my parents' story about my skunk running away couldn't possibly be true. I knew he loved me and wanted to stay. (Remember that "knowing" mode of communication...?) But parents would never lie to their children, right? And they certainly wouldn't take a beloved pet and abandon it alone in the woods, either, right? So you see my dilemma. I knew what I knew, but I was being told by my parents that my knowing was incorrect.

After a day or two, my skunk came home. Then he "ran away" again. That time, he didn't come home for over a week. The next time he disappeared, I could see him in my mind's eye, pacing along a riverbank, looking for a way across so he could come home.

I cried, howled. I begged my daddy to take me to look for my lost skunk.

I felt my skunk's desperation and sorrow as if it were my own. It was my own, in fact. I worried and cried and begged until someone finally spilled the beans: No one would be taking me to find my skunk, because he had been deliberately taken across the river and abandoned, so he couldn't come home again. Because back in those days no vet would attempt to de-scent a skunk, so he wasn't allowed to stay as my pet. My daddy had forced him to be free.

I was furious. My little five-year-old self was so furious I refused to speak to my daddy for weeks. I cried myself to sleep each night, haunted by the image of my skunk pacing the riverbank in desperation and fear. He'd been fed cat food every day of his life. Would he even know how to find food for himself? Or would he die walking that riverbank, trying to come back home?

I pled his case and mine, but my mother told me to stop being dramatic, stop being overly emotional. Of course I was just imagining things! How could I know that my skunk was pacing the riverbank? How could I know his feelings? Of course I couldn't, and of course a little girl couldn't keep a skunk as a pet.

My mother tried to convince me that my vision, my knowing, my feelings of the skunk's emotions, were my imagination. When I continued to argue, she warned me that it was disrespectful and hurtful for me to indulge in or talk about these fantasies. Finally, she accused me of "making-up stories" in a subversive effort to make my daddy feel guilty about doing the right thing. In other words, I couldn't trust myself, animal communication wasn't real, and talking about it was the same thing as lying. I was shamed into denying my abilities.

My animal communication abilities went underground after that. I reserved them for pretending during playtime with my dogs and cats and the wildlife near our house. I still brought

Lesson One: Thinking Back

home strays, but I didn't communicate with them anymore, except as a fun game of pretend.

Then in my early twenties, on a trip to Guatemala, I was taken by my host family to visit a local zoo. In that zoo was a circular waist-high wall. I leaned over to look into an eight-foot-deep concrete pit. A river otter leapt up at the side of the pit, pleading for help. I heard the words in my head, loud and clear: "Help! I'm trapped! Get me out of here!"

The poor creature was clearly not happy about being tossed into a concrete pit with no water to play in and no playmate to share his incarceration. Of course, I made an ass of myself, demanding that my bewildered host family help me find the person in charge of the zoo and tell them to release the otter. I had to be content—I wasn't—with writing a letter of protest to the zoo.

I remember the event vividly because the poor otter's desperate plea snagged my heart and never let go. But I didn't allow myself to think that the voice in my head might have been direct communication. I thought it was my overdeveloped sense of empathy (about which I'd been chastised all my life) giving an imagined voice to the otter.

Finally, in my thirties, I received a communication I couldn't deny. I was working part-time at a pet store because my kids were all in school, and I wanted a little job for extra money and something fun to do. I had a master's degree in education and a teaching certificate, but I wanted the flexibility of a part-time job so that either my husband or I could always be available for our kids.

Go ahead and judge me now for working at a pet store that sold purebred puppies. I judged myself for that, too. Before taking the job, I voiced my concerns about supporting puppy mills to the store's owner, and he convinced me that he had personally checked out every breeder that supplied the animals sold at the store. Because he also donated lots of window space for shelter puppies and kittens, I got over myself and took the job so I could spend my workday with animals. I rationalized that if I could help people choose the right animal companion for them, and then educate them on the care and training of their new family member, every animal that left our store would have a forever home, and I could feel good about that.

Weekends were always busy at the pet store, and on one particularly busy Saturday, I was hustling from one customer to another when a lady asked to see one of the puppies. Our store had small play rooms so people could get acquainted with the dog of their dreams before taking him home.

I had been exploring the idea of communicating with the animals at the store by pretending to ask each animal their name when they first arrived. Then, I pretended to hear their answer. (Pretending is a valid way to access your budding animal communication skills.)

Lesson One: Thinking Back

Naming the animals was against the rules, but I didn't particularly care about the rules. I'm not much of a rule-breaker, but I'm pretty good at bending them in half. ;-)

The woman had asked to see a precious little Cocker Spaniel that I hadn't yet held or "spoken" to. When I took the puppy from her kennel, she licked my face and sent a happy message: "Hi, my name is Millie."

I thanked Millie for sharing (silently, of course) and handed her over to the woman who was waiting in the play room. At this point, I was still thinking of this communication thing as a fun game of pretend. And I encourage that mindset if you need to allow yourself to explore animal communication without too much pressure.

Millie squirmed and whined to get back to me, and I knew she was trying to tell me something; but I didn't have time to listen. I assumed she might need to pee, so I handed the woman a towel in case Millie had an accident while they played. I left the woman and Millie alone for a few minutes, then came back to check on them. Millie was romping around the playroom. The woman was all smiles. Obviously, this was a match made in heaven, so I asked the woman if she wanted to adopt the puppy.

The woman's answer sent a chill through me. She said, "No. I only wanted to play with her because she reminds me of my dog, Millie, who died last year. Since then, I haven't had the heart to get another dog."

An immediate sense of knowing kicked me in the butt. Millie had told me her name so I could pass it on to the woman. But I'd missed the cue, and that was why Millie had been so upset when I handed her over to the lady without also saying Millie's name. If I had said, "This is Millie," the woman might have known that her dog had reincarnated in order to be with her again. That one nugget of information, delivered at the right time, might have made all the difference.

But once the woman said her old dog's name was Millie—validating my communication—the opportunity to share the information was lost. I couldn't think of a way to share the information without giving the impression that I was preying on the woman's deep emotional loss to make a sale. She walked out of the store without the puppy, and I had to believe that whatever healing the two of them needed had been accomplished in the five minutes they played together.

With that event, I finally accepted my gift of telepathic communication with animals. In one moment of validation, my most vivid memories of previous communications came out of hiding. I had to look at those memories of past communications and at least entertain the notion that they, too, had been real.

On my way home from work that day, I stopped at a book store and bought every book I could find on animal communication (there weren't that many). I started reading, learning, and practicing. I decided that since my communications with animals had been validated, I owed it to myself—and to the animals in my life—to learn how to access the gift at any time, rather than being blindsided by it.

At the same time, I had begun studying various forms of energy healing, and I met several professional animal communicators in the large community of healers in Houston, Texas (where we lived at that time). They encouraged and mentored me, and pushed me to put my own gifts out into the world so I could help others.

I also took every opportunity to attend classes and seminars, and was lucky to be able to learn from a renowned pioneer in the field of interspecies communication, Penelope Smith, before she retired. I made lasting friendships with some of the people I met in those classes, many of whom, like me, took her classes from the beginning level up through her last class for professional animal communicators and counselors.

My healing ability and my animal communication ability grew together and complimented each other. I became a Reiki Master and a certified Body Talk™ Practitioner. I learned Matrix Energetics and studied other healing helpers such as Bach Flower Essences, essential oils, and crystal healing.

In practicing my skills professionally, I found that animal communication made it possible to learn what my animal clients needed, and energy healing enabled me to assist in resolving any problems the communication revealed.

If you haven't already, I urge you to learn whatever forms of energy healing interest you, because while animal communication is a powerful tool for healing in itself, when paired with other forms of energy healing, it's nothing short of miraculous. If the accounts of communication and healing that you read in this book don't convince you, you'll soon have stories of your own that will.

I hope that my story has encouraged you to embrace your own latent skills of animal communication. I assure you that with the knowledge you acquire reading this book, combined with diligent practice, you can become adept, and even masterful, at telepathic animal communication.

LESSON ONE HIGHLIGHTS

🐾 Most people have communicated with animals without knowing it.

🐾 Well-meaning parents and authority figures often shame a child into abandoning their gift of animal communication.

🐾 As a child's abilities "go underground," some memories of their communications with animals will be forgotten; others will be mislabeled as imagination.

🐾 Once an adult reclaims their ability to communicate telepathically with animals, some of those buried memories may resurface.

🐾 Pretending is a valid way to access your budding animal communication skills.

🐾 Energy healing is a good complement to animal communication.

Hear Them Speak

LESSON ONE TASKS

1. Buy a composition book. Don't get a spiral-bound notebook because the pages will fall out before you finish the course. Don't get a nice hardbound blank book, because you may be subconsciously afraid of messing it up. You'll be writing your communication transcripts in this notebook. You'll be journaling your experiences, making notes of validation, and of when and why you may have been "off." You'll be flipping through the notebook to track your progress. You'll be carrying the notebook around a lot. By the time you fill it up, it will be battered and well-worn. If the cover of the cheap composition book offends you, you can decoupage it with inspirational images and quotes.

2. Get some nice writing pens and a set of highlighters: green, red (or some other color if red seems too mean for marking possible mistakes), and yellow.

3. Set aside an hour of practice time every day for the duration of this twelve-week course. Pick a time when you're least likely to be disturbed. If you can't devote a whole hour, get as close to that as you can. During the practice time you have set aside, you'll communicate with one animal each day, and take notes longhand, with your very nice pens, in your notebook. One day, you may graduate to typing your

notes on your computer, but writing longhand accesses a part of the mind that typing does not. Automatic writing is a great device for tapping into your abilities. You'll find, especially in the beginning, that writing longhand primes the pump for communication to flow.

4. Set aside some time for daily meditation. If you're not used to meditating, you may have to start slowly to keep from being frustrated. If you're a meditation newbie, use a guided meditation audio so all you have to do is find a quiet place and listen. Start with five minutes a day, then work up to twenty minutes, or longer if you have time.

5. Contact some trusted friends and ask if they'll allow you to communicate with their animal companions. Even if you have plenty of your own animals to work with, you'll soon need to branch out. Even more important, in the beginning, you will need to validate, from an outside source, that the information you're getting is accurate. Working with animals you don't know well (but someone else does) is a great way to do that.

6. Something to remember: You aren't confined to working with animals who are still present on the earth in physical form. Animals who have crossed over into spirit can still communicate quite effectively. Animal communication is a

heart-to-heart, spirit-to-spirit connection. A physical body isn't required.

7. Think back through your childhood and try to remember any past experiences that could have been animal communication, even though you may have dismissed them as your imagination at the time. Write about these memories in your animal communication notebook. Include any times when you felt an emotional connection with an animal, or felt your own emotions changing in response to your proximity to, or thoughts about, a particular animal.

8. Write about any times you can remember when, as a child, you pretended you could talk to animals. Could it be possible that you really were communicating?

9. Write about any times when you were shamed or chastised for communicating with animals—or even for talking about it. If you can't remember any childhood communications, don't judge yourself. You may have blocked some memories, or you may simply have forgotten communications that were dismissed at the time as unimportant. Buried memories may surface long after you've completed this course.

LESSON TWO: Laying the Foundation

In this lesson, you'll learn about the different modes of communication, a brief overview of how it feels to receive each of these modes, and some common blocks that can keep you from receiving clear communication.

Figure 3: *While this book will give you the guidance and tools you need to communicate, animals will be your teachers. Ask them to help you, and they will.*

Anyone can communicate telepathically with animals. Some people have more natural ability than others, just as some animals are better communicators than others. But anyone with the desire to communicate and the commitment to practice can learn.

To get you practicing as quickly as possible, this lesson will provide a quick outline of the different ways communication may be received, some common blocks to communication, and important tools to help you become a clear channel for your innate telepathic abilities.

Don't worry if you feel the need for more explanation; we'll delve deeper into theory in subsequent lessons, and many of the questions you have now will be answered when you experience telepathic communication for yourself.

How is Telepathic Communication Experienced?

Telepathic information is experienced through the subtle senses, which are an extension of the five senses we learned about in elementary school: *seeing, hearing, feeling, tasting,* and *smelling.* The sixth telepathic sense we'll discuss in this book is *knowing,* a more global way of understanding that we often call intuition. This can give us much more information than the simple gut reaction of good/not good that we feel when presented with certain people or circumstances. We will also explore other, non-telepathic avenues of information-gathering that are useful, such as *observation*. While any source of information is fair game when it comes to helping us understand a situation, it is important to remember that these other sources of information are not telepathy.

Figure 4: *Observation can help you tell when an animal is ready to communicate. Animals who are communicating telepathically often look as if they're in a deep trance or about to fall asleep. Notice that Todd the fox isn't looking at me; he is focusing on an inner landscape of memory that he is conveying to me through images, words, and feelings. Some animals will communicate while they're looking at you or even noodling around the room. But when you see this "inner focused" expression, you can be sure the animal is doing its part to connect. Photo by Therese Clinton.*

While observation can be helpful, it can also masquerade as telepathic information if you're not careful. Anyone can observe an animal's behavior or expression and come up with an opinion of what's going on. You will learn how to separate your observations and opinions from the telepathic information you'll receive, making yourself into the clear channel through which it flows.

You will also learn how to send telepathic information through that same clear channel.

It is interesting and fun for humans to learn how to listen to animals. But it's often life-saving when we can help animals understand what humans expect of them. For an animal communicator who is dedicated to making a difference in animals' lives, learning to receive telepathic information from an animal is only the first step.

Figure 5: *This precious puppy ended up at the animal shelter where I volunteered and practiced my animal communication skills. Even animal companions with perfect pedigrees and exemplary behavior find themselves in shelters; they show up in need of help, understanding, and the kind of counseling that only animal communicators can give. Some are lost; others simply didn't fit in with the family as expected. Situations change, and people change their minds about what's most important to them. Human companions die or move away. For a multitude of reasons, perfectly good friends-for-life are abandoned, left alone to wonder why they have been discarded. Many animals who are surrendered to shelters have no idea why they weren't allowed to stay with their families. Most would have done anything to stay in the homes they'd thought would be theirs forever. If only they'd understood what was expected of them, things might have been different. Animal communicators are in a unique position to save the world, one forgotten, misunderstood animal at a time.*

How Does it Feel to Receive Telepathic Communication?

🐾 **Visual information** can appear as a snapshot or a short movie clip that enters the communicator's mind. Receiving this sort of information feels like remembering a specific moment in time, or visualizing a character or scene in a book you're reading.

🐾 **Auditory information** is like hearing a voice in your head. Often the voice will come through with a distinct accent or way of speaking. Some animals will use more formal language than others. Some will be almost poetic in their use of words; others will give short, to-the-point answers. Personality and attitude come across clearly though auditory communication.

🐾 **Feeling information** can be "felt" as a physical sensation in the body or as an emotion. This type of information can feel subtle or overwhelming.

🐾 **Smell information** can come as the memory of a scent, or you can experience it directly as a scent that appears during the communication and then dissipates.

🐾 **Taste information**, similar to smell, can come as a memory or a direct experience. (Be careful not to ask an animal to show you how their favorite food or treat tastes. Some animals enjoy eating poop.)

🐾 **Knowing information** happens when an animal gives you access to their memory or knowledge in a way that bypasses the five subtle senses. This feels like remembering a book you've read or a course you took in school. You have the holistic knowledge of an entire event, or even a lifetime, available to you in an instant.

🐾 **Observation information** isn't telepathy. But simply observing what is right in front of you can be a valuable tool in digging down to the truth of a situation. Observing the animal's behavior, environment, and relationships can enable you to ask the right questions in a telepathic conversation. So, while observation shouldn't be confused with telepathy, it is included in the savvy communicator's toolkit. When you're out to save the world, you have to be prepared to access any tools that present themselves.

You will often receive more than one of these modes of communication at a time. You may find that some modes are easier for you than others. Acknowledge your strengths and weaknesses, but don't get locked into a mindset about what you can and can't do. If receiving visual information isn't easy for you, keep an open mind. With time and practice, it will get easier.

Like people, individual animals will have individual communication styles. Some prefer to send visual images, while others will be more verbal. Some will send information faster than you can write it down. Others will be silent until you ask the perfect question. And some animals simply won't be interested in communicating with you—at least, not at the time you're attempting to connect. So if you try to communicate with an animal and get no response, don't assume it's your fault. The animal may simply not care to interact with you right now. If this happens, say "thanks anyway," and move on. Try again another day, and you may find that the animal is ready to talk.

Or, it could be that you've asked the wrong question. You won't know until you try a different question—or two or three—and see what kind of response you get.

Telepathic communication arrives via the subtle senses.

The subtle senses are an extension of your five senses: *seeing, hearing, feeling, tasting, and smelling. Knowing* is another telepathic sense (think of it as intuition on steroids) that can give a global understanding of an animal, its history, or a situation.

Lesson Two: Laying the Foundation

Remote vs. In-Person Communication

In-person communication requires you, the communicator, to be in the same physical space as the animal (I know I didn't really have to explain this).

Remote communication involves connecting with an animal through a photograph or description provided by the animal's human companion.

Working with animals remotely can sometimes be easier than communicating in-person. Some animals are so determined to receive physical attention (playing ball, getting petted) that they'd rather do that than communicate with you. Some situations aren't conducive to good communication because other things are happening, or other animals are demanding attention. In these instances, you may have better luck connecting remotely.

Then, there are times when communicating in-person can be more helpful than connecting remotely. Sometimes, the home environment and observed interactions between family members can yield important information that isn't as readily available through remote communication. While these observations aren't telepathy, they can help you to ask the right questions.

By the end of this course, you will be able to communicate both in-person and remotely. It's important to practice both so you don't get stuck thinking you are only good at communicating under certain circumstances. No psyching-yourself-out allowed!

How Do I Know I'm Getting Real Communication?

You may not be able to tell the difference between telepathic communication and your imagination at first. That's okay. At first, you may have to *fake it till you make it*. That's okay, too. It may help to adopt the attitude that for now, you're just pretending to communicate with animals. If you're a perfectionist, an attitude of playfulness can relieve the pressure of perfectionism so you can allow yourself to explore your abilities in a non-threatening way.

Over time, and with practice, you will learn how it feels to receive accurate information and how to tell when you're projecting your own thoughts, feelings, or opinions into the conversation. You'll become adept at checking your own filters and being aware of clues that you're on track (or off base).

Until then, there is great freedom in learning and using these statements:

🐾 I'm just practicing.

🐾 I'm still learning.

🐾 I could be wrong.

🐾 I could be full of shit.

Lesson Two: Laying the Foundation

Especially in the beginning, when you are still learning and practicing, you will sometimes be wrong. Even when you're an animal communication whiz, you might sometimes be wrong. Or, you could be right, but people may think you're full of shit anyway. There is no profit (or point) in trying to convince anyone that animal communication is real, or that the information you've received is correct. Proof is convincing. Nothing else is.

When you're communicating with someone's animal, all you can do is get whatever information you get, relay it to the best of your ability, and let the person make of it what they will. Often, someone who insists that you're dead-wrong today will call tomorrow to relate the amazing story that proved you were right.

I once got a call from a woman who was convinced that her old dog hated the new puppy and was very jealous of the attention the new puppy was getting. The evidence of this theory was that the old dog barked and growled at the puppy whenever the woman picked it up.

I made a house call and was met at the door by a middle-aged woman who cradled a tiny, button-eyed Schnauzer puppy in her arms.

The old dog, an arthritic-looking spaniel mix, padded into the entry hall and sat at my feet the moment I walked in the door. She told me that she loved the new puppy. She wasn't jealous. She was worried that the woman would spoil the puppy with over-pampering and ruin its presently good nature. What seemed like jealousy was the older dog's attempt to discourage the woman from turning an innocent puppy into a little tyrant.

The woman led me to the living room and invited me to sit. Once we were seated, I asked the woman to put the puppy on the floor and see how the older dog interacted with it. She clutched the puppy to her bosom and declared that she didn't dare put the baby down where the jealous older dog might attack it.

This was early-on in my professional animal communication career, so I didn't insist that the woman release the puppy right that minute while I was sitting there. Instead, I told her everything the older dog had said, then suggested that she stop carrying the puppy around all the time, and instead put it on a flexible schedule that included playtime with the older dog and alone time or naptime in a crate. I explained the need for the puppy to have positive interactions with many dogs and people so that she didn't become overly dependent on one person to the exclusion of all others.

The woman paid me for my visit, though while she wrote the check she grumbled that what I'd "come up with" made no sense. I folded the check and put it in my pocket, promising that I wouldn't deposit the check unless she called me within the next few days and told me to.

She called me before I'd even made it home, and told me to deposit the check. She had put the puppy and her older dog together in the back yard as soon as I left her house, and they were still playing and running circles around the place. She didn't believe in the truth of the communication until she saw the resulting change in her dogs' behavior for herself.

Plenty of people will doubt you. You will doubt yourself, too, and that's a good thing. But the more validation you get over time, the more you'll begin to realize that yes, you are really communicating telepathically with animals.

Some Common Blocks to Effective Communication

Strong emotion is probably the biggest block to communication. And of the strong emotions that block communication, the biggest is fear. Fear of being wrong, fear of looking foolish, fear of being judged, fear of what you may learn, fear of being the only person in the universe who will never be able to communicate with animals no matter how hard you try.

Fear works both ways—an animal who is fearful is also going to have a hard time communicating. An animal who is lost and can't find his way home isn't likely to be a terrific communicator.

Think of someone making a 911 call. They may not be able to remember their address, or describe what is happening accurately to the operator. Stress hampers the ability to think clearly.

Other strong emotions that can block communication are love, pity, frustration, anger, guilt, grief, and worry, to name just a few. Even an overcommitted calendar can block your ability to receive clear communication. If you're worried that your house is a wreck and you've just learned that company is about to arrive, you won't be very good at communicating until you clean the house. Sometimes, you will have to TCOB (take care of business) before you can settle in to receive telepathic communication.

Often, it comes down to mindfulness of your own situation. Are you ready to be a clear and neutral vessel through which communication can flow? If not, why not? What do you need to take care of before you can communicate?

Figure 6: *As an animal communicator, you must be a neutral, empty vessel through which telepathic information can flow. Strong emotion, opinion, or personal agenda can hamper this. Even thinking, Awww, she's so cute! Can keep you from experiencing the depth of wisdom an animal has to offer.*

Lesson Two: Laying the Foundation

If your heart is swelling with love or pity, or even, *Awwww, she's so cute*, you aren't neutral enough to be sure that your own feelings aren't coloring the communication. We all—animals and humans—see life through our own filters. But in the space of communication, it is a communicator's responsibility to remain neutral. Or, if that isn't possible, ask another communicator for help or validation. If it isn't possible to confirm with another communicator, remember the phrase, "I could be wrong."

Especially when you're first beginning to practice, it can be harder to connect with your own animal companions than with animals you've never met. This happens because our emotions are so intricately entwined with those of our loved ones. If you have trouble connecting with your own animals, start with non-threatening subjects such as likes and dislikes, or opinions about favorite places and foods and activities rather than emotionally charged subjects.

Figure 7: *This is Jack, our three-legged Best Good Dog and Most Benevolent Pack Leader during his tenure here. In this photo, he was in his prime, and the two of us communicated easily. But toward the end of his life, my fear of knowing how much he suffered physically kept me from communicating with him effectively. My emotional attachment made it hard for me to accept the message when he wanted my help to cross the Rainbow Bridge. I didn't want to let him go. Jack was also conflicted. He had been abandoned by his previous "family," who moved out and left him chained to a tree in the empty back yard. (Healthy at 60 pounds, he weighed 18 pounds when a neighbor noticed him and set him free to stagger into the road and get hit by a car.) His lifelong fear of abandonment made it difficult for him to make the decision to cross the rainbow bridge, because he knew he would have to do it alone. Strong emotions on both our parts made clarity hard to achieve.*

Lesson Two: Laying the Foundation

Our emotions can block us from receiving clear telepathic information. The animal we're communicating with may also have emotional blocks that keep them from being good communicators. Even the projected emotions or agendas of the animal's human companion can block or cloud communication between "their" animal and a communicator. The person can be yearning so desperately to hear what they want to hear, or be so fearful of hearing something they don't want to acknowledge, that they can actively or subconsciously block clear communication.

A man asked for my help with his dog's strange behavior. The dog barked hysterically whenever anyone, even the man or his wife, arrived or left the house. The odd behavior had begun to escalate into dangerous territory; the dog now attempted to nip at anyone who walked or stood near the front door.

When I received the client questionnaire and photos of the dog, the photos were all dark and blurry, and the client's questions were geared toward blaming others: "Were you abused by your breeder before you came to our house?" and "Does Mommy..." (meaning the man's wife) "...make you nervous?" and "Is our other dog mean to you?" It seemed that my client was so invested in hearing that the dog's problems weren't his fault, that he was actively trying to steer the conversation in a certain direction.

I knew something was up from the minute I read those questions and saw the dim, blurry photo that could have been a dog, or a toddler in a Wookie Halloween costume.

Hear Them Speak

I asked the man to please send photos that were candid, clear, and taken in sufficient natural lighting. But every photo he sent was as bad, or worse, than the last. I finally decided that nothing better was forthcoming and went with what I had. When the dog didn't respond to any of the questions the man had provided, I tried asking some open-ended questions like "Why do you bark when anyone enters or leaves the house?" and "What makes you nervous?" and "What would make you feel more relaxed and calm?"

Even those questions got less than complete answers.

I called the man to admit defeat, but he wasn't home, so I wasn't able to speak with him. Instead, I got an earful from his wife. According to her, the dog's only problem was that her husband—who'd enlisted my help in the hope that I would prove him right and her wrong—had turned the dog into a nutcase.

I asked what she meant by that, and she explained how her husband had attempted to train the dog to be a good watch dog by faking extreme fearfulness whenever anyone showed up at the house. When the dog's reinforced behavior finally escalated beyond tolerable limits, the man refused to accept responsibility and hire a professional dog trainer (an idea the wife had suggested) to correct the problems he had caused.

Poor dog. No wonder he had problems. I refunded the money I'd been paid, recommended professional behavior training for the dog, and wished them all the best of luck. I felt bad for the dog, and hoped the woman in the household would be able to convince her husband to get professional help in retraining the dog. Otherwise, the dog's behavior would continue to escalate until living with him became unbearable, and he would eventually be euthanized. I don't know what happened, ultimately, in this situation.

Sometimes you can help, and sometimes all you can do is shake your head.

Another Block to Communication is Your Opinion

Some common opinions: Animal-lovers shouldn't eat meat. Dogs shouldn't live outside. Cats should never be allowed outside. Birds shouldn't be kept in cages. Wild animals shouldn't be tamed. It's wrong to confine animals in zoos or aquariums. Animals such as carriage horses or police dogs shouldn't be made to work. People shouldn't breed purebred dogs when so many mixed breeds are being euthanized.

These are all valid opinions, and you are entitled to yours. However, your opinion, your sense of how things should be, has no place in telepathic communication.

Try not to *should* on people, whether they are animals or human. (Animals are people, too.) Some dogs like to live outside. Some cats hate being confined indoors. Some birds love their cages. My Solomon Island Eclectus, Ruby, feels safe in her cage and will only tolerate short visits out of it. A little cuddling and attention for Ruby goes a long way.

Figure 8: *This is our Solomon Island Eclectus, Ruby. She feels safe in her tidy little cage; too much open space makes her feel exposed and vulnerable. When we tried to move her into a larger cage, she sat in one corner and squawked until we gave her back the sense of security she needed. Though the other birds enjoy spending time in the outdoor aviary when the weather is nice, Ruby hates it and can't wait to come back inside.*

If you allow your opinions to enter the communication, you are doing a disservice to the animals who depend on you to relay *their* thoughts and feelings, not yours.

I will admit that when I first started communicating with animals, I had the opinion that dogs are happiest when living indoors with their human companions. Most of the time, this is

Lesson Two: Laying the Foundation

true. Dogs are hard-wired to live in a pack, or family, and if they are stuck outside by themselves while the rest of the family is indoors, they can become stressed-out, destructive, and antisocial. But I have since met many dogs who prefer living outdoors. I had to ditch my opinion and understand that every dog—every being on this planet, in fact—is an individual, with individual preferences.

The first dog who helped me to understand the mentality of an outside-only dog was named Oliver. (You'll hear more about his story when we dig deeper into the block caused by opinions.)

When I asked Oliver if he wanted to live inside the house with the rest of his family, he said, "I love my human family, and I know that they love me. But their life is busy and hectic, with so much coming and going and stressing over every little thing. I prefer to be outside with my family of squirrels and birds in the yard. I like to be able to lie in the sun during the day, and look up at the stars at night. I know that I am the first line of defense for my human family. People with bad intentions see me in the yard and walk past. I am proud that I can do that for my people. They love and appreciate me, and I feel that I am doing what I was put on the earth to do."

One of our own dogs, Jed, feels this way. He doesn't get to sleep outside at night, because I don't allow that, and he has to abide by my rules. So, like many dogs—and people—he has to compromise to get along.

My compromise is to let Jed go outside for an hour or so before bedtime. He patrols the perimeter, and assures himself that everything is as it should be. Then, at bedtime, Jed takes up his protective position on the couch by the windows. This way, if anyone were to approach our property, he would know about it.

Another Block to Communication is Circumstance

If the animal you are trying to converse with is begging for treats or attention, you won't get anywhere. It is even worse if the animal is afraid, hurt, or in danger. Any animal—even a human animal—has a variety of needs that must be met before communication can occur.

According to Abraham Maslow's Hierarchy of Needs, biological and physiological needs including water, food, shelter, and sleep, must be met before second-order needs, including safety and freedom from fear, can be considered. Communication would come under the third hierarchy of needs that include trust, acceptance, belonging, intimacy, and love.

Animals whose basic needs haven't been met may not be able or willing to connect with you for telepathic communication.

This doesn't mean that you absolutely won't be able to communicate with an animal under these circumstances. In fact, an animal in dire straits may reach out to you when you're not even paying attention. Like the otter who called out to me for help, animals in need may be the ones to prompt a conversation.

Lesson Two: Laying the Foundation

When "It's **not you**; it's me."

Your own situation will impact your ability to communicate. The situation that is blocking your ability to communicate might be environmental (maybe you are in the middle of a hectic place where there's a lot going on) or internal (your body, mind, or emotions are busy coping with something other than communication).

The first step in blasting through these blocks is to identify when they are happening. Then, you'll be able to take steps to minimize or erase them.

When working with an animal in-person, you will need a relatively quiet space (in your mind, if not in reality) and the animal will need to be receptive and attending to the conversation. Easier said than done, and some highly distractible animals may not be able to settle down enough to communicate. If this happens, don't get frustrated. If the animal's human companion will allow you to connect-in remotely later, get their contact info and take a photo of the animal with your phone. Then, when you're in a quiet space without distractions, you can chat with the animal and follow up with their human by phone or email.

Working remotely, you'll require a quiet space and a quiet mind to receive clear communication. If your kids are turning cartwheels around you and your spouse is asking where the TV remote control is, you are unlikely to get anywhere. When the external environment is the problem, you may have to go somewhere else or wait for another time when there will be less interference.

Figure 9: *Gregory the goat might have something important to say to Lambert the ram, but Lambert's mind is on something else. If your brain is churning, you'll have a hard time creating a calm, empty mind-space for communication to enter.*

Lesson Two: Laying the Foundation

A Too-Busy Mind is a Block to Communication

You will have to learn to quiet your mind. To do that, it is essential that you meditate often. You may not be the incense-burning, candle-staring type, and that's fine. Find a kind of meditation that works for you and use it. Find a moving meditation like swimming or walking. Try chanting mantras, knitting, or making pottery. Many physical or creative activities will allow your mind to float just-enough to derail your hamster-on-the-wheel thought processes, allowing you to find the silent spaces between your thoughts. The more you go to that quiet place in your mind, the easier it will become to access at will.

A Clear Mind Fosters Clear Communication

Because a regular meditation practice helps to clear the mind and balance the emotions, it is one of the most important tools in the animal communicator's toolkit. If you have a meditation practice, please keep it up. If you've fallen off the meditation wagon, now is a good time to get back on. If you've never meditated before or haven't found a method that works for you, I've included additional material about meditation in the appendix.

Your spirit, your mind, your body, and your heart are the vehicles in which telepathic communication travels. Take care of them, and they will help you receive clear communication. Nurture your spirit, enrich your mind, nourish your body, and cherish your heart.

Have compassion for yourself—say no when you need to, sleep when you're tired, eat when you're hungry—and you will have more capacity to extend that compassion to others. Take time for yoga and meditation. Make time to spend in nature, absorbing the wisdom and peace of the trees. Go to the beach and immerse yourself in the waves—figuratively if not literally. Sit in your own garden or porch for ten minutes on a busy day.

You know these things, I know. But just in case you need it, I'm giving you permission. In fact, if you need more than permission, I'm happy to command you: Treat yourself well so you will maintain a deep reservoir of strength and peace that will nurture and empower you.

It isn't easy, but it is simple. We all have within us the seed ability to communicate telepathically with animals. We can choose to nurture and grow that seed or let it lie dormant. If you follow through with this twelve-week course, and give it 20 percent of your focus and attention for that small length of time, you will germinate and fertilize the seed until it grows into a thriving ability, the scope of which you can't even begin to imagine now.

Twelve weeks out of a whole lifetime, devoted to learning what you already know deep inside, can change everything.

Can you do it?

Yes, certainly.

Will you?

Lesson Two: Laying the Foundation

That's completely up to you.

I hope you will. I hope you'll complete the entire course, because the world needs more animal communicators. In fact, the world as we know it can't survive without us.

LESSON TWO HIGHLIGHTS

🐾 The subtle senses are an extension of your five senses: seeing, hearing, feeling, tasting, and smelling.

🐾 Knowing is another telepathic sense that can give a global understanding of an animal, its history, or a situation.

🐾 We learned how it feels to receive each of these modes, and some common blocks that can keep you from receiving clear communication:

- 🐾 strong emotions or opinions
- 🐾 external circumstances
- 🐾 the animal's human
- 🐾 higher-order needs
- 🐾 a too-busy mind.

🐾 We learned that we can communicate in-person or remotely, and that there are drawbacks and benefits to each.

🐾 We learned that while observation can help us to ask the right questions, observation is not telepathy.

Lesson Two: Laying the Foundation

LESSON TWO TASKS

1. Meditate—or at least try to; there's a reason they call it a meditation *practice*—for a little while each day. Shoot for one or two twenty-minute sessions, or start with five minute sessions and build up to twenty minutes. Of course, more is better, if you have time. If you've never meditated before or haven't found a method that works for you, read the appendix on meditation and choose a method to try.

2. Now that you've read about the ways that telepathic information is experienced by the receiver, think about whether you may have been communicating with animals without realizing it (or times when you thought it may have been happening but weren't sure). Write about any instances that cross your mind, even if you don't remember how the information felt when you received it. Has your dog ever reminded you that the water bowl was empty?

3. Think about times when any of your animal companions may have heard your thoughts and reacted accordingly. Has your cat disappeared when you were planning a vet visit, only to reappear after you called the vet to reschedule for another day? Writing about our experiences often helps us to mine those experiences, to dig deeper, recall more, then dissect and reassemble those memories into something meaningful that

will help us move forward. Write about those memories and see what comes up.

4. Thinking of common blocks to communication, can you identify any that might apply to you? Are you afraid of how you may have to rearrange your life if you accept your ability to communicate with animals? Are you worried about what your loved ones, friends, and relatives will say? Write about any potential blocks that come to mind.

5. Imagine a situation (or a few) in which someone asks you some pointed questions about animal communication. What is animal communication? What is telepathy? Why are you learning about it? How do you square the idea of animal communication and telepathy with your (or their) beliefs? What will you say? Write out a few possible answers. Sometimes, we don't know what we think until we write about it. What do you think about telepathic animal communication?

6. Do some research on energy healing, and find a modality that interests you. Maybe make plans to take an energy healing class after you've finished this course.

LESSON THREE: Getting Started

In this lesson, we'll dive into the practical application of what we've learned so far. You'll try your first practice session this week. But first, it's important to address boundaries, etiquette and safety.

Figure 10: *In this photo taken by fellow animal communicator Therese Clinton, I'm kissing Sweet Boy, a deer who can't live in the wild because he was captured as a fawn and neutered when his antlers were just beginning to grow. I don't have to wonder if he yearns to be free, because I can converse with him and know that he is happy and well cared for since wildlife conservation authorities brought him to Jungle Exotics sanctuary. To have the opportunity to get this close to animals that aren't usually domesticated, you have to understand when it is safe and appropriate to interact with an animal, and when it isn't.*

Boundaries

Boundaries are about knowing what is your responsibility and what isn't, what is your business and what isn't. It's about you keeping *yours*, and letting everyone else keep *theirs*.

One way to keep good boundaries is to only go where you're invited, either by an animal's human or an animal who initiates a conversation. If an animal in need asks for help (like the otter in the zoo who leaped up and yelled [telepathically] to get my attention), that's an invitation. If your attention is caught by an animal who is abandoned, abused, or in peril, that's an invitation.

If you happen to pass a dog and his human out for a walk, that's not an invitation. Not to anthropomorphize, but think of animals who are out and about with their human companions as little children. If an adult human started a conversation with a small child who is accompanied by his parent, that wouldn't be welcome. That would be creepy. Animal communication is definitely a superpower, but if you put on your tights and cape and start accosting people and their animals, you won't be thanked. You'll probably be arrested for indecency.

Be mindful of privacy issues. It's best to use a list of questions provided by the animal's human unless you've been given permission to explore any topic or the animal has offered information or asked you for help. Even healing energy should not be given without first receiving permission from the animal.

Lesson Three: Getting Started

Another important boundary is the emotional boundary between you, the animal, and the animal's human. You will encounter many emotional situations. You will hear about things that will hurt your heart or make you angry. Don't let the emotional things you hear and see become a part of you. I can tell you how damaging this is because I've done it myself.

If you're not careful, you can take on the emotions of others, so much so that you lose sight of the boundaries between your emotions and someone else's. Anyone who has ever worked (or lived!) with someone who is angry and frustrated knows how difficult it is to keep your own emotions on an even keel when you're surrounded by someone else's drama. In this lesson, you'll learn how to protect yourself from internalizing or processing the emotions of others.

We'll also discuss how to manage your own emotions. One thing that helps with this is to manage your expectations. As an animal communicator, you will experience miracles of healing and connection that you can't begin to imagine. But you will also learn that you can't make everything in the world bend to your will.

While you can help animals and their human companions, you can't control their universe. This may be a hard realization for some people to grasp, but here it is: You can't fix everything. You will save yourself a lot of heartache if you recognize that while your animal communication skills may indeed solve many problems, you aren't expected to be a fixer-of-everything-for-everyone.

You can give an animal's human companion some of the information they need to make important decisions about their animal's welfare, but you can't make those decisions for them. If you tried to exert your will or promote your opinion in the decision-making process, you'd be overstepping an important boundary.

Even when you're asked to make—or influence—such decisions, please remember that boundary, and politely say no. Eventually, you will be asked to change an animal's mind about their end-of-life plan. People with the best intentions have asked me to heal animals who were too sick or too emotionally or spiritually damaged to be healed. While the humans wanted to do everything in their power to turn back the clock, the animals were tired of suffering, and the only thing to do was to let them go.

There will be times when you'd like to help, but aren't able to because your overture is rejected by the animal, or the circumstances just won't allow it. I've tried unsuccessfully to catch dogs running loose on the highway, eventually admitting defeat and leaving them behind knowing that they'd soon be hit by cars and left to bloat in the summer sun. I've driven past dogs chained to doghouses in the dirt, knowing that because no law was broken, there was nothing I could do. Could I, should I, have tried harder? Done more? Will that question torment me forever, or can I let it go?

Lesson Three: Getting Started

One way to protect your emotions in these situations is to say a prayer for the animal, or send a healing intention that the animal's spirit is free to accept or reject. Then, knowing that you've done something, at least, you can release your own emotions and move on. Whenever I drive past an animal that's been killed on the roadway, I always send this healing prayer: *"May your trauma be released and your spirit raised to its highest vibration."* I always feel a lightening in my own soul when I do this, and I can usually tell that the animal's spirit has been assisted, as well.

It took me a while to learn the importance of keeping good emotional boundaries; I learned by making mistakes. I've grieved for the pain and loss of animals beyond my reach, and kept that grief inside me instead of processing it and letting it go. Making up for those I couldn't help, I adopted animals who may have been better served by being euthanized.

Help when you can. But when you can't, please don't take these failures into yourself. Don't be a psychic sponge. Recognize when you, yourself, need support. Keep your own heart safe when you're trying to heal the hearts of others.

Etiquette

Always introduce yourself and ask if an animal wants to speak with you before diving into a conversation. If the animal's human has provided a list of questions and concerns that seem serious, start with some lighter conversation first. Then, at the end of the conversation, always thank the animal.

Be respectful of an animal's time, space, and privacy. Don't assume that they'll want to tell you everything—or anything—about their life. Sometimes, you'll have to gain their trust before they'll want to share anything with you.

Physical Safety

Don't assume that an animal wants to be touched, even if they are communicating with you. Working from a safe distance is best for you and for them. Wild animals will often communicate quite easily with you, as long as they know you're not trying to trap or tame them, but that doesn't mean they want to cuddle. Even tame animals will often communicate more to a person who isn't also trying to connect on a physical level. Super-affectionate animals can be so focused on getting petted that they're not interested in communicating at the same time.

Keep your distance from an animal unless they—and/or their human—invite you to come closer. If you do get an invitation, use your good judgment about whether to accept it. Humans may not understand what their animal companion wants, likes, dislikes, or is capable of. You can communicate and send energy healing just as effectively—or even more effectively—from a distance.

Lesson Three: Getting Started

Figure 11: *This sweet kitty wanted me to come inside her enclosure and pet her. I asked whether she would bite. Her response: "Only if you try to leave." Photo by Therese Clinton.*

I've tamed many feral cats who were caught in live traps (and some who just showed up here at Dragonfly Pond Farm knowing that they would find help). Many of these wildings wouldn't consent to engaging in telepathic communication until they were mostly-tame. And they certainly wouldn't have welcomed my touch.

When taming a wild animal, you are pushing against the boundaries that keep them safe. You are finding the edge of their comfort level and gently moving past it. But that kind of pushing isn't conducive to communication. You can push for proximity, or you can communicate. You can seldom do both at the same time.

Psychic Safety

Animals will teach you many things about the workings of the universe. I've met animals who are healers and psychics and otherworldly beings. I've met others who've been haunted by restless spirits or troubled by entities.

There are things in this world that we cannot begin to understand. And not all of them are nice. You really don't have to worry about all this, at all, if you remember to maintain good boundaries on all levels—physical, emotional, mental, and spiritual.

Absorbing emotions and energies that aren't yours can affect you adversely (think about a time when you were impacted by the drama and strife of others and you'll understand what I mean). So, it is important to practice good psychic and emotional hygiene.

Before beginning your communication session, take the time to set good boundaries.

First, set the intention that your energy will remain with you. Be mindful not to leak or project your own energy or opinions onto others. Even when you're sending healing energy, be careful that it's only coming through you, not from you. You can be a channel for healing energy, but you don't want to deplete yourself by sending your own personal energy to someone else.

Next, set the intention that you won't absorb or invite any energy (emotional, psychic, or otherwise) that isn't yours.

Lesson Three: Getting Started

There are many ways to do this, but it really is all about setting your intention in a way that resonates for you. There's an appendix with more information about psychic safety at the back of the book if you want to learn more before you get started, and I encourage you to flip back and read through it. But for those of you who are already well-informed about this subject, here's a quick and effective way to get centered, cleared, grounded, and protected before beginning a session:

Centering: Close your eyes, lean back in your chair, and put your feet flat on the floor. Be aware of your body, release any tension, and focus on your breath.

Clearing: Breathe in, from the soles of your feet to the top of your head. On the in-breath, you're absorbing strength and calmness from Mother Earth. Breathe out, sending down anything you don't need for Mother Earth to lovingly transform. Visualize yourself emptying of everything that could get in the way of pure communication.

Grounding: Imagine that your feet are growing roots that will anchor you to the core of the earth.

Protecting: Set the intention or say a prayer to keep yourself safe from any external influence.

Figure 12: *Asking for protection can be as simple as, well, asking for it. Your prayer or request or intention is yours alone; make it as spare or as elegant as you like. Inked art by Tessa de Jongh*

A Few Last Words before You Start Practicing

First, I want to let you know what to expect, what *not* to expect, and what to do when you ask a question and get a heaping helping of nothing.

Don't expect every animal to start communicating right away. Animals aren't inclined to chatter, because they don't stay in output mode the way most people do. Their minds are quieter than ours, not whirling with thoughts and opinions and plans and worries. Animals are generally content to inhabit their bodies and

Lesson Three: Getting Started

experience the moment-by-moment unfolding of their lives rather than living in their heads as people do. When you first connect with an animal, be ready with a specific question, rather than expecting them to inundate you with a bunch of unsolicited statements about how they feel and what they think.

Don't expect every animal to help you ask the right questions. Their rules of communication aren't the same as ours. If you're talking with a person and you ask a question that's a little off base, they'll correct your question and then answer the revised question.

Example: You ask a person you've just met where they work. They say, "I don't work anymore, because I retired last year, but I was an elementary school teacher for twenty years. Now, I volunteer three times a week at the animal shelter."

See how a person—in output mode as most of us are—revised the question and then answered it, plus adding more information that wasn't asked for?

Animals will usually ignore a question that doesn't pertain to them. If you ask an animal a question that's slightly off base, they'll wait quietly for you to come up with a better question.

Example: You ask a cat whether he likes his bed, when he doesn't care about his bed one way or another—in fact, he has no idea what that round cushion you're referring to is for. He won't inform you that you're asking a question that isn't relevant to him. He simply won't answer. Or, if he does understand the question but doesn't give a flip, he may give a terse yes or no answer but won't volunteer anything more.

It is good to start with specific, open-ended questions. Instead of "Do you like your bed?" ask, "Where do you like to sleep?"

But even then, when you've asked an open-ended question about a subject the animal doesn't care about, you're still likely to be met with silence. What to do?

> **Better questions get better answers.**

Once, a client wanted me to ask why his dog was "fickle" about being petted. I asked the question, using the client's wording, and got nothing. I reworded slightly, asking the dog why it seemed that she didn't like being petted. Again, no answer. So I tried to come up with something more open-ended that didn't assume how the animal felt.

When I asked, "How does it feel to be petted?" I got an immediate sensation of my skin crawling, like it was super-sensitive to touch. I also got an image of the dog's skin rippling, much the way a horse's skin does when it is shaking off flies. It wasn't that the dog didn't like being petted; she wanted the love and attention. But her skin was so sensitive that too much petting was uncomfortable. I did some energy healing to calm down her over-reactive skin, and my client reported that the next time he petted his dog, she allowed him to stroke her back for a much

Lesson Three: Getting Started

longer time than usual. Immediately, she became even more accepting of touch, and over time, she became so comfortable that she asked to be petted more often.

When you're coming up with your questions—or finessing the questions provided to you by the animal's human—try to use open-ended questions, and don't assume how an animal feels.

When I took my first advanced-level animal communication class from Penelope Smith (whom I mentioned earlier—she is an expert in the field of telepathic animal communication), she provided the class with a list of great questions to use when communicating with animals, especially when you're first beginning to practice. The questions Penelope gave us encouraged me to dig deeper in my conversations, to get past unimportant details and into more meaningful territory. Penelope has given me permission to share her insightful questions:

Hear Them Speak

1. What have you to teach me? What can I learn from you?

2. What do you like about being a (type of animal)?

3. What is your favorite activity? Greatest joy in life?

4. What is your favorite food?

5. How old are you? (Years/months/weeks, sense of seasons of life, or you may get date of birth)

6. Who are your friends? Who is your best friend?

7. What do you like about your environment?

8. Is there anything you would like to change about your living situation?

9. Is there anything you'd rather be doing?

10. Do you have any physical problems or ailments? Tell me about it: Where does it hurt, and how does it feel? What can we do to help you?

11. What is your viewpoint about humans? About me?

12. What is your purpose(s) in life?

13. What do you dream of?

14. What can you tell me about your past? Your future? Your present?

15. What do you see as my purpose?

16. What haven't I understood about you? Please explain.

17. What don't you understand about me? Explain to the animal.

18. How can I improve my telepathic communication with animals?

19. How can I help you in any way?

20. Is there anything else you wish to tell me?

Thank you!

©1984 Penelope Smith; shared with permission.

Lesson Three: Getting Started

Ready to Start?

I know that some of you are impatient to start practicing, and others may be getting nervous about it. In either case, the cure is to go ahead and give it a whirl. Think of this as a trial-run. If it doesn't work, no worries, we'll delve deeper and learn more theory as we go along. As with anything, the effort you put into it will determine the experience you'll get out of it.

Practice with your own animals, of course, but enlist the help of your friends and their animal companions, too. Even better, ask your friends to refer their friends to you, so you can work with animals you don't know well, and with people who will be willing to validate the answers you have received.

Especially at first, don't ask for a lot of background information, because you don't want to begin a telepathic conversation with any preconceived notions. The animal's name and a description or photo are enough.

Before you begin the conversation, just sit with the animal (or its photo or description if you're working remotely) and allow them to send any information they'd like to share. They may share images or words, emotions or energy, or something else. Be open to whatever you receive. Write it down, acknowledge it with gratitude, and remember that it's a conversation, not an inquisition.

The animal may have questions for you. Animals who have never experienced telepathy with a human may be surprised and want you to explain what you're doing.

Your first questions may be dictated by what the animal shares with you, and after that you can pick and choose from the list of questions in this book or given by the animal's human. If a question doesn't quite work out or give you the full story, modify it or ask a different question. Allow the conversation to flow naturally, using the questions given here as a guide, but not a formula. Be creative in your questioning; be willing to follow the conversation where it leads, and be ready to dig deeper than the first, surface answers.

If you're not sure of the information you have received, ask for clarification. "I think I heard you say _____. Is that right?"

Or, "I'm seeing a picture of _____. Did you send me that picture?"

Or, "Am I asking the right questions? Is there something else you'd rather talk about?"

And if all else fails: "Am I doing this animal communication thing right? Can you help me?"

This is not a contest.

It ain't deadly-serious.

It's a fun exploration of what-ifs: What if all you have to do is relax and accept? What if it is easier than you thought to change the world? Don't let the fear of being a superhero derail you. The

Lesson Three: Getting Started

world will not stop spinning if you don't succeed before you even start.

Take it easy.

Allow, don't strive.

This is easy, unless you make it difficult.

Humility Opens the Door to Understanding and Power

Figure 13: *I took this photo on our travels in Florida. Pelicans are powerful, but humble. They are much larger than you'd think, and not to be trifled with. (Beware that beak! Mind those wings!) Strong and capable, pelicans don't care what anyone thinks of them. Meek and unassuming, they don't feel diminished when they need to ask for help (or a handout). Pelicans understand that there is strength in humility. They know their potential, they are open to possibilities, and they accept their limitations. Be a pelican.*

Now It's Your Turn!

We will begin our practice with remote sessions, so you can concentrate on the experience without the distraction of a live animal who may have an agenda beyond communicating (such as being petted or getting treats).

We will be digging deeper into each of the modes of communication in the next few lessons, so don't worry if your first session is less than inspiring. Think of it as a trial run. Even if you are not immediately successful, it is important to practice the beginning steps of connecting with an animal.

Lesson Three: Getting Started

Quick Start Guide: Short Directions for Remote Communication

1. Find a quiet place where you will be undisturbed.

2. You will need the animal's name and either a good description or a clear photo that shows the animal's eyes. You'll need your notebook, a pen, and a list of questions.

3. Expect to have fun! Remember, this is an exploration, not a challenge.

4. Close your eyes and take a few slow, deep breaths Use the time to get centered, grounded, and protected.

5. Imagine the animal you'll be talking with. See them coming up to you and giving you their attention. When you can imagine that vividly, you are *in*. Introduce yourself and ask the animal if they are willing to communicate with you.

6. Write your first question out longhand in your notebook. Ask the question in your mind, then close your eyes and wait to receive. The answer may come as words, an image, a feeling, a taste or smell, a sense of knowing, or a combination of these things.

7. Give yourself time to receive. While telepathic communication is immediate, you may need to wait for your initial blocks to dissolve. If you are a kinesthetic person, the act of writing will help, so feel free to write the question over again, or just doodle until the answer arrives.

8. Write what you get without judging. If you don't understand what something means (images are especially open to interpretation) ask for more information, or ask them to repeat their answer.

9. If you don't get a response, move on to another question. Silence on the animal's end of the conversation does not mean you are doing something wrong.

10. At the end of the session, be sure to say thanks!

When You Finish a Communication Session

Validate everything you get with the animal's human. Don't hold back on telling what you get, even if it seems strange. The human may know what it means. I once talked with a horse who showed me an image of a pair of women's high-heeled shoes when I asked about his favorite things. I almost didn't tell this to the horse's human because it seemed too strange. But I did decide to tell, and I was glad I did, because it turned out the horse had special, expensive horse shoes with an elevated heel to help with a medical condition that made him lame.

Make notes when you talk with the animal's human. Note when you were right and when you were "off." Over time, you'll learn how it feels when you are on-target and when you are projecting your own thoughts and opinions.

I still have my first animal communication notebook. Battered and worn, its handwritten notes contain some of my favorite animal communication tales.

Now, you will be collecting your own amazing animal communication stories! Open your mind and your heart, and buckle your seatbelt. You have just embarked on an amazing journey.

Lesson Three: Getting Started

LESSON THREE HIGHLIGHTS

🐾 One way to keep good boundaries is to only go where you're invited, either by an animal's human or an animal who initiates a conversation.

🐾 Before beginning a communication session, take the time to set good boundaries. Set the intention that your energy will remain with you and that you won't absorb or invite any energy that isn't yours.

🐾 Always introduce yourself and ask an animal if they will be willing to talk with you. Always thank them after the conversation.

🐾 Be mindful of privacy issues. It's best to use a list of questions provided by the animal's human unless you've been given permission to explore any topic or the animal has offered information or asked you for help.

🐾 Be respectful of an animal's time, space, and privacy. Sometimes, you'll have to gain their trust before they'll want to share anything with you.

🐾 Though we will focus on remote communication in the beginning, you may have opportunities to communicate in-person with some animals. Remember that working from a safe distance is best for you and for the animal with whom you are communicating.

- 🐾 Don't expect every animal to be a gregarious extrovert. You may have to gain their trust before they will open up. It may help to tell them that you are practicing and would appreciate their help.

- 🐾 Better questions get better answers. Ask open-ended questions and don't assume you know the answer.

- 🐾 After each session, get validation from the animal's human.

- 🐾 Have fun! An attitude of playful exploration will help you to open up to your abilities.

Lesson Three: Getting Started

LESSON THREE TASKS

1. Have a remote telepathic conversation with a different animal each day, during the hour you've set aside for practice. Make note of the time you communicate with each animal, as well as any time during the communication that you seem to lose their attention. The animal's human may be able to validate that the animal's behavior was different during the communication, or that something happened during the time the animal was distracted from your communication.

2. If possible, validate the information you've received with each animal's human. Make notes on any further information you are given.

3. Using your highlighter pens, mark the information that was undeniably correct in green.

4. Mark information that couldn't be validated but may be correct, or partially correct, in yellow.

5. Flag information that couldn't be validated but seems to be incorrect (or straight-up wrong) by making a small red line in the margin beside it. *Don't mark through it!* Often, information we think is incorrect is just a little left-of-

center, or it requires us to dig deeper, or we've received the correct information but have interpreted it incorrectly. Sometimes an animal's human will shoot down something one day and then remember or realize what it meant the next day.

6. If you have more red than green and yellow, don't judge yourself. We'll deal with those red lines later on, and you may be pleasantly surprised that you weren't as *off* as you thought.

7. A few days after you have validated each communication session, have another conversation with each animal's human and see if anything has changed. Has the animal's behavior changed? Has the human noticed anything new or had any realizations about the information you gave them? Make notes in your notebook.

8. If you would like the support of fellow students who are working through this book, as well as graduates of this course and my in-person workshops, please visit TinyURL.com/HearThemSpeakClassCoffeeshop. Once there, click Join Group to be approved by an admin. In the group, you'll be able to ask questions and mentor each other along, and I'll pop in regularly to help out, too. See you there soon!

LESSON FOUR: Visual Information

In this lesson, I will give specific examples of what it looks and feels like to receive visual information, and summarize key points to help you remember them. By the end of this lesson, you will understand the many ways visual information can be experienced.

Figure 14: When I communicated with Zuma, he showed an image of himself rolling in hay, and another of getting his mane brushed. He was jealous of a special needs lion who got more attention (and hay, and hair-brushing) than he did. Not understanding the reason the other lion got so much coddling, he claimed, "I can do anything better than him! He's not as great as he thinks he is!" A couple of days after I left the sanctuary, Zuma was granted both of his wishes. My friend sent videos of him playing in a pile of hay then getting his mane brushed. It was so gratifying to see the expression of bliss on his face! It takes such simple things to make an animal happy. Photo by Therese Clinton.

Hear Them Speak

How to Tell You're Getting Accurate Visual Information

Receiving visual information feels like remembering a specific moment in time, or visualizing a character or scene in a book you're reading. A visual image can be literal, or it can be a figurative representation of something similar. The image may be from a viewpoint that humans wouldn't usually see.

🐾 Visual information can appear in your mind as a snapshot or short movie clip.

When I communicated with Zuma the lion, I was sitting in front of his concrete-floored enclosure. I asked him what his people could do to make him happy, then closed my eyes to receive his answer. An image popped into my mind. It came through as a short movie clip that showed him rolling in a big pile of hay.

I thanked him for his answer, and then asked, "Is there anything else they could do to make you happy?" He showed me a snapshot image of his keeper brushing his mane.

> When you get an answer from an animal, don't assume it's all they have to say on the subject. They may have a laundry list of answers that are just waiting for someone to ask the right questions! Follow up any question—and especially the end of the communication session—with this question: *Is there anything else you want to tell me?* Keep asking "Is there anything else?" until they say "No, that's it."

Lesson Four: Visual Information

🐾 **One way to tell that the visual you're getting is on-track is when the image is surprising, something you didn't expect.**

At an American Kennel Club (AKC) dog agility event, a woman wanted me to ask her dog if he missed anyone. The dog moved closer to the woman and laid his head on her knee. At the same time, he showed me a picture of a bed—not a dog bed, but a four-poster bed with a rumpled blue or gray bedspread. Clearly, a bed isn't *someone*; it's *something*. It wasn't the visual I was expecting, but it was a clear image. I didn't see the bedroom it was in, or even the pillows on the bed. Just a bed with a blue-gray bedspread.

Rather than trying to get more information or ask to see more of the picture, I told the woman, "I don't know what this means, but he's showing me a bed with a blue or gray bedspread." The woman slumped in her chair and covered her eyes for a moment. Then, she stroked the dog's silky head and told me that her husband had died in that bed just a few months before.

🐾 **Sometimes, the visual image you see in your mind's eye won't be a complete scene like you would find in a photograph. Sometimes, you will only see one item with no background, like a flash card.**

The dog who showed the image of a bed showed only the bed, and nothing around it. He didn't show anything of the bedroom, because none of that was important. He showed me a flash-card image of a bed and nothing else.

Remember my story about the horse with the high-heeled shoes? He also showed a flash-card image of something surprising: a pair of bright red stilettoes.

🐾 An accurate visual image is usually clear, at least in part.

While you may not see all of a picture, complete with background detail, at least part of the image will be clear. The edges may be blank like a flash card or hazy and dark as you would experience in tunnel vision. There may be "missing" pieces, like an incomplete puzzle. But the important part of the image, the part the animal is trying to convey, should be clear.

You may sense that there are some parts of the image that you can't see, but as you dig deeper into the conversation, the missing elements around the clear central image may emerge.

You may also notice that the "camera angle" changes from a wide-angle view to an up-close view to one that shows a scene from the animal's perspective.

🐾 An accurate visual image often shows the animal's viewpoint. It's as if you are seeing a movie through the animal's eyes.

Lesson Four: Visual Information

I once spoke with an Australian Shepherd about some of his behaviors that his human wanted to curb: He liked to jump up to greet people, and he had a tendency to wander beyond the boundaries of the family's unfenced rural property. When I addressed these issues, I could tell he was feeling fussed-at. He threatened to check-out of the conversation, so I tried to redeem myself by asking a fun question. "What would you be, if you couldn't be a dog?"

What had been a dull, frustrating conversation for both of us suddenly perked up.

"I'd be a fish!" He showed himself sitting on the grassy bank of a well-stocked fish pond, looking down into the water and watching the fish swim. The image showed only the dog in the center of the frame, the pond in the foreground, and a grassy bank rising up behind the dog. I had the feeling that there was a house in the distance, just over the hill I could see on the horizon, but the house wasn't within the frame of the image.

The dog's human hadn't told me how large the property was, or whether it had a pond. But I knew I was receiving an accurate image, because it was so clear, almost like looking at a snapshot or painting. My only worry was whether the image I was seeing was of a pond on the family's property, or whether the pond had lured the dog to wander outside his boundaries.

When I asked the dog whether the fish pond was on his land or the neighbor's, he responded, "It's all mine!" Dogs have a somewhat different idea of property lines than humans do. (Luckily, it turned out that the pond was on the family's land.)

"Why do you want to be a fish?" I asked. In reply, the dog showed me a movie clip of himself wading into the pond. The camera's view tightened, then shifted to show the experience through the dog's eyes as he looked down into the water. I could feel his intense interest in the fish swimming around him, coming within a few feet of him, but no closer. His reflection on the water's surface quivered with excitement and wonder. But whenever he tried to get closer, the fish moved away. Teasing, tantalizing, tempting, but always keeping a safe distance from their curious friend. The only way to know more about fish, he'd decided, was to become one.

> When you dwell on difficult topics in a telepathic communication, the animal may shut down and refuse to continue the conversation. Be sure to vary your questions and explore fun topics as well as serious ones so the animal doesn't feel that he's being verbally attacked.

Lesson Four: Visual Information

🐾 The visual image may be accompanied by other modes of reception (such as feeling and knowing in the next example).

A friend had just moved into a new house, in a new neighborhood. She had kept her cat inside for couple of weeks, but then the cat insisted on going outside, so my friend finally relented and opened the cat door to the outside world. Then, the cat disappeared for more than a week, so my friend called me.

The cat showed that she was hiding in a small, closed-in space. I was given the image of a dug-out space under the porch of a house built on a pier-and-beam foundation. I also had the *feeling* of damp mustiness. I had the *knowing* that the cat wasn't hiding under the new house, but she wasn't far away, either. The cat told me in words that she was "creating a new grid around the neighborhood." Not a grid of protection, exactly, but more a grid of belonging. She was somehow putting down energetic markers in a circumference around the house.

🐾 The image you see may be from a viewpoint you would not normally be aware of as a human.

When the cat showed a picture of herself hiding under the porch in a nearby house, I saw strips of light shining through the porch's floorboards onto the packed dirt right where she was crouching. I didn't see the house, or the surface of the porch. No potted plants, no rocking chairs, no visual of the exterior of the house. I was seeing purely from the cat's viewpoint rather than what a human would be aware of.

She also sent an image of a king-sized bed with the faint markings of sandy cat-footprints on the bedspread, along with the knowing that she often crept through the cat door to sleep at the foot of my friend's bed during the night.

My friend checked her bedspread and saw the faint, sandy residue of her cat's overnight sleeping space. Relieved that her cat was nearby, doing her own thing and coming home when she needed to, my friend relaxed and waited for the cat to reveal her presence when she was ready. A week later, the cat came home for good, apparently satisfied that the neighborhood was safe, and the family now belonged there.

Lesson Four: Visual Information

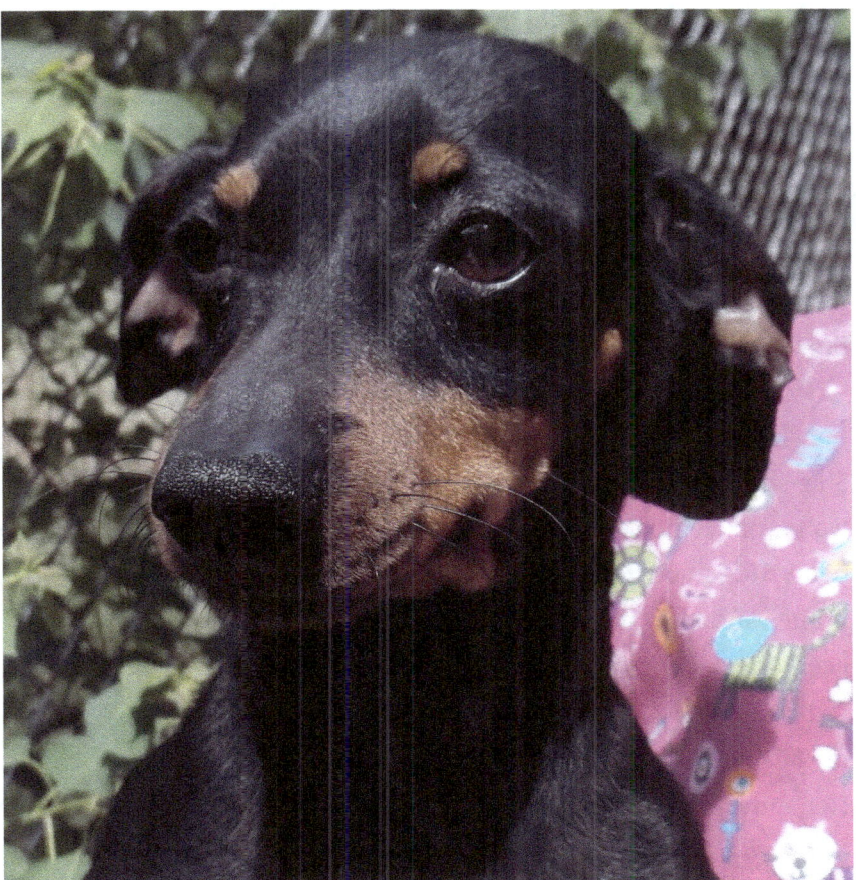

Figure 15: *A small dog, afraid of being stepped-on, may show an image of the only thing she can see clearly from her viewpoint. There won't be faces, or any part of the humans other than a towering forest of legs and larger-than-life feet that she has to avoid.*

🐾 **An animal may give a figurative representation of an object, event, or state of mind rather than a literal image.**

I spoke with a cat whose human was a friend of a friend. I didn't know the person or the cat. I didn't have a photograph to work from. No background information was given beyond the cat's name and description, and the question: "Is Fluffy ready to die?"

I figured Fluffy must be old or sick, but when I connected with her, I felt a sense of youth and serenity, not of age and suffering. She showed an image of a spacious cathedral of light with no walls or ceiling. Pillars of colored light moved through the beautiful space. I was made aware that the cathedral was Fluffy's home, and the pillars of rainbow-colored light were her people, each one a different color.

It was obvious to me that Fluffy was blind, but she didn't live in darkness. She could still see light, shadow, and energy fields. Her mind—or heart?—had assigned colors to each person in her family, so she had no trouble telling where her people were, or where she was, in her home environment.

When I spoke with Fluffy's human, she told me that the previous year, Fluffy had had a seizure that resulted in blindness. Fluffy's person was happy to know that Fluffy still enjoyed her life and wanted to stay, even though she couldn't "see" in the traditional sense of the word.

Lesson Four: Visual Information

A cat may show herself wearing a crown and sitting on a throne to represent her position in the household. A dog may show himself flying with wings to represent how it feels for him to leap over the bars in an agility trial.

Another time, a woman asked how one of her dogs felt about the other dog in the household. The dog being asked the question showed the image of a large bulldog, standing in an assertive stance with his chest puffed out. I relayed the image to the woman, and she said that while her other dog wasn't a bulldog, that large-and-in-charge attitude with the chest puffed out and prideful was an accurate representation of how he conducted himself.

Knowing that visuals may not always be literal, make sure you let people know this up-front, especially before you share an image that doesn't make perfect sense to you. Then, when you tell them what you see, they'll be thinking not-just of literal interpretations, but of other possibilities such as mannerisms, states-of-being, or a representation of something else.

Non-literal images can also be helpful in accurately diagnosing a physical problem

Figure 16: *It is easy to observe from this photo that Charlie the cheetah feels bad. When I asked, "Hey, Bud, what's wrong?" Charlie showed me an image of a green beach ball swelling in his belly. Had Charlie somehow swallowed a beach ball? No, of course not. But he felt bloated, and green is the universal color for nausea. Charlie couldn't tell me (because he didn't know) what had caused his discomfort. But knowing what the problem was, Charlie's caregivers at Panther Ridge were able to treat Charlie's intestinal upset and then do some detective work to find out which food had caused the problem. Photo by Anne-Laure Michelis.*

Lesson Four: Visual Information

🐾 You may experience a visual of colors highlighting a certain part of the body, or your attention may want to "stick" on one part of the body.

Visual information about physical or medical problems can come as a haze of color, a non-literal image (like Charlie's green beach ball) or a finely detailed literal image of an actual physical body part. When I think there may be more detailed information available than what I'm seeing at first "glance," I will sometimes pull up an anatomical study (on my computer) of the sort of animal I'm communicating with, and see where my attention wants to stick. Then I can dig deeper by asking to see colors, or areas of darkness, or whatever I decide would best illustrate whatever ailment my intuition tells me I'm searching for.

Just to be clear: when I'm "seeing" colors or whatever, I'm not actually seeing the image change color on my computer screen. I'm not seeing the image change, at all, with my physical eyesight. I'm allowing my intuition to show where the image *would* change if I *could* see it with my eyes. A couple of times, I have seen psychic information with my physical eyesight. It looked like a translucent image overlaid on what was really there. But the image was fleeting and not the sort of thing you should expect to see often, if at all.

You can use your intuitive sense of sight like a built-in X-ray machine. A good way to access this visual scanning method (if it doesn't happen automatically) is to close your eyes, and set the intention that when you open your eyes and look at the animal (or an image of the animal) your attention will be drawn to any part of the body that isn't healthy or in balance. Or, you can set the intention that any part of the body that is inflamed will look red, any part of the body that is in pain will look black, etc., assigning colors for whatever issues you are trying to pinpoint.

Again, don't expect to actually see the animal change colors! It's more a feeling of, *if I could see a haze of color that indicates a problem, where would it be?*

Now, you have a good understanding of the subtle sense of sight and how it works. You understand by now that it's usually perceptual rather than visual. A hologram doesn't appear; a movie-screen doesn't pop up out of nowhere. It's an image, still or moving, that comes into your mind through your imagination.

How cloudy or clear that image appears can depend on how cloudy or clear your own mind is. And you're still meditating every day, right? Because the more you meditate, the more you will become a clear channel for receiving telepathic information.

How detailed or complete an image you receive is can depend on your ability to receive, but it may also depend on the animal, and on what information is most important for you to see.

Lesson Four: Visual Information

LESSON FOUR HIGHLIGHTS

🐾 Visual information can appear in your mind as a snapshot or short movie clip.

🐾 One way to tell that the visual you're getting is on-track is when the image is surprising, something you didn't expect.

🐾 Sometimes, the visual image you see in your mind's eye won't be a complete scene like you would find in a photograph. Sometimes, you will only see one item with no background, like a flash card.

🐾 An accurate visual image is usually clear, at least in part.

🐾 An accurate visual image often shows the animal's viewpoint. It's as if you are seeing a movie through the animal's eyes.

🐾 The image you see may be from a viewpoint you would not normally be aware of as a human—up a tree, in the sky, under water, etc.

🐾 The visual image may be accompanied by other modes of reception.

🐾 An animal may give a figurative representation of object, event, or state of mind rather than a literal image.

🐾 You may experience a visual of colors highlighting a certain part of the body, or your attention may want to "stick" on one part of the body.

Lesson Four: Visual Information

LESSON FOUR TASKS

1. Meditate daily even if just for a few minutes.

2. Continue practicing daily telepathic conversations with different animals, getting validation from the animal's human whenever possible, and making notes. If you're having trouble getting settled enough to allow your abilities to flow, try connecting-in during a different time of day.

3. Using your highlighter pens, underline correct info in green, maybe-or-partially-correct info in yellow. Flag seemingly-incorrect information with a red line in the margin (don't strike through the words).

4. Write about your experience so far. Are you feeling successful? Stuck? A little of both? Write a few pages, longhand, stream-of-consciousness, as quickly as you can without stopping to overthink. Have any emotions or internal conflicts surfaced? Have you invited any drama into your life in a subconscious effort to slow or derail your progress?

5. In your writing, explore any visuals that came up for you in practice this week:

a. Did you receive any surprising visual images during your communications this week? What was that like?

b. Did you receive any images that pinpointed only one small area? Why do you think the animal only showed you a small-focused area?

c. Were your images clear, or hazy, or clear in some spots and hazy in others? How did these communications feel? What was your mindset when you received clear images vs. when the images seemed hazy?

d. Did you get any flash-card images?

e. Were any of the images shown from the animal's viewpoint vs. the view of an outside observer? (Such as a kitten seeing the view from under the porch vs. a human looking down at the kitten.)

f. Did you receive any images that were from a strange viewpoint? (Underwater, underground, the sky?)

g. Were there any non-literal images? (Red stilettos = horse shoes.)

6. Celebrate! You deserve it! Go out and do something fun!

LESSON FIVE: Auditory Information

In this lesson, I will give specific examples of what it looks and feels like to receive auditory—aka verbal—information telepathically, and summarize key points to help you remember them. By the end of this lesson, you will have a firm grasp of the many ways auditory information can be experienced.

Figure 17: *Even a rattlesnake can be as eloquent as any poet: "I have lived near your house and watched you from a distance, keeping a respectful space so as not to cause you fear. I am both humble and powerful. I have great love for all things. I am not violent or cruel. I help animals who are ready to transform into spirit, striking quickly and accurately so they don't suffer. I assist them with love and reverence for their life and spirit, and I experience their transformation along with them. Their bodies as food are a gift back to me for my loving help with their transformation."*

How to Tell You're Getting Accurate Auditory Information

Receiving auditory (or verbal; I will use the terms interchangeably) information is like hearing a voice in your head. It is similar to the way you imagine a character's voice in a book you're reading, or the way you remember a voice you've heard before. Often the voice will come through with a distinct accent or way of speaking. Some animals will use more formal language than others. Some will be almost poetic in their use of words; others will give short, to-the-point answers. Personality and attitude can come through clearly with auditory communication.

🐾 **Accurate auditory information, like accurate visual information, is often surprising, something you** didn't **expect.**

This happened when one dog said of another dog in the family, "She's very nervous in her body." That's an interesting way of putting it, not the way I would think or imagine, but it fit the personality and expression of the dog who had sent that verbal communication.

It also happened when I talked to a parrot that I had every reason to think was a male, but when I opened the conversation with, "Hi, Felix," he answered in a huffy, *Housewives of Atlanta* accent and attitude, "It's *Felicia*."

Lesson Five: Auditory Information

Figure 18: *Felicia's personality and attitude came through clearly with auditory communication. A voice can also come through with a distinct accent or way of thinking. When an animal communicates with a particular accent or personality, you know you're on target. Photo by Celia Lambert.*

Felicia, the parrot with a *Housewives of Atlanta* accent and attitude, belonged to a couple who are friends of mine and my husband's. Celia and Joel's Felicia had a sassy, southern style of speaking. Her accent, attitude, and word choices showed a great deal of individual personality.

Before the conversation, we already knew that Felicia adored Joel, who treated the bird with a casual, offhand affection. But she was quick to bite Celia, the woman who fed her, cleaned her cage, and wanted to foster a loving relationship.

I asked Felicia why she was so mean to Celia.

Felicia said, "Celia is one woman too many, no offense. That man is mine. No offense, nothing personal. That's just the way it is."

Celia and Joel also had a dog with a distinct voice and personality. In fact, all of their animals are exceptional individuals, probably because Joel and Celia are, too!

Hazel, an elderly Rat Terrier with a short, sleek coat, claimed to be the reincarnation of a turn-of-the-century schoolmistress. She had taken on the task of tutoring all the other dogs in "proper comportment." She seemed to view herself as a governess for the family. She showed herself as a prim-and-proper woman with graying pin-curls. I asked why she'd showed me the pin-curls, because Hazel's hair was short. She let me know that one of the other dogs, a black Pitbull-mix named Soot, kept messing up Hazel's hair.

Soot was too slobbery and undisciplined for Hazel's liking.

She said, "Please do tell Celia and Joel that I'm so happy to have met them and shared their home. I will do my utmost to help Soot. Sometimes I despair, but when she settles a bit, I may have some luck."

Lesson Five: Auditory Information

Figure 19: *Hazel's prim-and-proper way of speaking reflected her personality. A school teacher at heart, she felt obligated to tutor the other dogs in the family in "proper comportment." Photo by Celia Lambert.*

🐾 **Accurate auditory information will often come through in a way that sounds like the sort of conversation you're used to having with humans.**

Animals who answer right away with words will usually keep the conversational ball rolling smoothly, often answering the next question before you ask it. It's an indication that you're getting good information when the animal is responding with words and/or images faster than you can type or write their responses.

Highly verbal animals are often wise counselors who have come to help their human through a difficult time, or to assist them along their path toward self-actualization. Don't be surprised if the puppy or kitten you're conversing with sounds more like an ascended master.

You've heard about people having guardian angels. Sometimes those angels have fur and claws instead of wings.

Two-year-old Australian shepherd, Max, had a lot of sage advice to give his person: "Tell Eric that he is exactly where he is supposed to be right now, and he can stop working such long hours to feel worthy of success. I can help him learn to let go of the things he's trying so hard to let go of but at the same time hold onto. I can show him how to sit with emptiness and wait with patience. I can show him how to accept joy when it comes, without trying to grab it and make it stay. I can show him how to empty his heart of all resentment and anger, and when it has sat empty for a while, joy will come to fill it. If he will sit with me, I will show him how to be at peace with himself and the world."

Now, you might imagine that telling a client (someone you don't know well, if at all) something this personal is a little awkward. I didn't know anything about Eric's past, his anger and

Lesson Five: Auditory Information

resentments, his fears and worries. I didn't know what Eric did for a living, much less whether he worked long hours. For all I knew, Eric could have been retired or disabled. But part of trusting yourself as an animal communicator is being willing to relay what you get, completely and faithfully.

You might be wrong.

But you'll never get good at this unless you own what you get, whether it turns out to be right or wrong.

Eric had come to me, not because he was looking for psychoanalysis, but because of his dog's inappropriate peeing (Max peed on Eric's shoes on a fairly regular basis). But animals know their human companions better than you do. So if an animal asks you to share information, you can trust that the human will understand. Max had specifically said, "Tell Eric," so that's what I did. I sent the transcript of the message exactly as I'd received it.

As an animal communicator, every single time I send a transcript to a client, I'm going out on a limb. I'll admit to being afraid of heights, but I've learned to live with the discomfort. I've learned not to look down when I hit the "send" button.

Worst thing that could happen? I could be wrong.

The antidote for that fear? Just go ahead and admit it.

The more consistently you can admit to the possibility that you could be wrong, the quicker you'll get to the point that you seldom are.

When I spoke with Eric after the session, he validated everything Max had said. Eric did work long hours, and he admitted that he was holding onto resentment and anger about a recent divorce. In a follow-up a week later, Eric reported that while Max had stopped peeing on his shoes, he still had accidents on the screened porch. When I checked in with Max again, he said that while Eric was better about spending more time with Max and paying attention to him on the weekends, he still worked late hours during the week. Max promised that once Eric started behaving better, so would he.

🐾 Auditory information that isn't easy to obtain may still be right.

Accurate auditory information will often seem as natural as having a conversation with an old friend. But it isn't always that easy. If you have trouble getting auditory information, that doesn't mean it's wrong, or that you're doing anything wrong.

Some animals prefer to send visual images. When you ask primarily visual communicators for verbal clarification, it will often come as short, one-word answers, and getting those answers may feel like you're "pulling teeth."

I once asked a fancy, furry little dog if she had any physical problems she wanted to tell me about. She showed me a visual of her fluffy little paws. I asked if her feet hurt, and she said no. I asked if she had anything stuck between her toes, like a thorn or a sand-spur, and she said no.

I asked if her toenails needed to be clipped, and she didn't answer. But she hadn't said no, so I thought maybe I was on the right track and just needed to dig deeper. (Notice how not getting an answer was a clue!) Finally, through a series of questions, I got the message: the little dog wanted—no, *needed*—to have her toenails painted. When I told this to her human, the woman validated that she had been so busy that she had rescheduled several appointments with the groomer. The fancy little dog who was accustomed to having every whim fulfilled before it had even been expressed was feeling very neglected.

I've also spoken with animals whose standards were so low from their previously difficult lives that they were thrilled to live in a home where clean water and food were provided on a daily basis. Every animal, every situation, is different. The better you are at setting aside your own opinions, the clearer you will be at hearing what each animal wants you to know about them, their lives, and their needs.

🐾 **You know you're getting accurate verbal information when the other animals in the household give corroborating testimony. Or, they may disagree, but provide a reason.**

Remember that humans and animals alike see life through their own filters. Their belief systems and life experiences color the way they perceive things. So even though animals aren't as inclined to lie as humans are, they may disagree on the facts of a situation.

When I talked with three Maltese dogs, their human wanted to know which of the dogs had been peeing on the bedroom floor.

Pinkie's prompt answer was "Bluebell."

Bluebell was the most expressive and verbal of the three dogs. She defended herself; "I only peed in the kitchen. I got excited and did it by accident. Abby is doing it in those other places because she wants to go outside."

I asked Bluebell why Pinkie had blamed it all on her.

"Pinkie is worried about getting in trouble," Bluebell said. "She doesn't know who did it. She is very nervous in her body."

I asked the culprit, Abby, to tell me what was going on.

Abby told me, in a mix of images, knowing, and words, that she was full of unexpressed energy. She needed more exercise and more time outside. She insisted that she was using her only weapon (peeing where she shouldn't) to let her human know that she would prefer going outside to do her business. In her opinion, potty-pads (which were always available for her use) should be reserved for rainy or cold days. She asked to be taken on more walks, by herself, without the other dogs. She wanted to be seen as an individual, not just one of the "dog-collective."

Lesson Five: Auditory Information

🐾 **When auditory information is paired with visual information, it is easier to be confident that both are correct.**

My client also wanted to know why Bluebell "walked up his body" at night, which kept him from sleeping. She answered, "It is quiet then, and everyone else is asleep, and I can have him all to myself."

Bluebell showed an image of herself hanging back and politely waiting her turn for attention, then sometimes not getting it. "I want attention, too," she said, "but I'm not going to put myself forward when everyone else is there. If he will just pet me a little and let me sleep next to him," she continued, showing a picture of herself curling up to sleep after a few minutes of petting. "I won't keep him awake. I don't want to be forgotten just because I'm quieter than the others."

Bluebell's way of using visuals and words at the same time made her communication clear and easy to understand, more than either visual or auditory answers alone would have done. When communication comes this way, it's much easier to know that you're on-target.

Animals who use equal parts visual and verbal communication will tend to give longer verbal answers, along with more detail, and they will toggle easily back and forth between visual and verbal, or use both simultaneously.

🐾 **It's a pretty good indication that you're getting accurate verbal information when an animal gives an opinion that opens a window into the** animal's **worldview.**

I once spoke with an elderly pair of dogs who were both opinionated and outspoken, like two old ladies who enjoyed arguing amiably and dissing each other. Lucy claimed, "I'm not a dog, I'm a movie star! I'm the princess, and Ethyl is the pea."

Ethyl had less to say, but her personality still came shining through. "Lucy is such a diva," she said. "She thinks she's all-that, always wanting to be the center of attention, always a hypochondriac, limping around like she's in pain. She needs to quit complaining. She needs to use it or lose it."

🐾 **Hold onto your hat, but** it's **also a pretty good indication that you're getting good verbal information when an animal tells you something that challenges your worldview or gives you fresh—or even astonishing—insight into the workings of the universe.**

You'll find that animal communication is much easier when you approach it with an open mind. Your belief systems may be challenged by some of the things you hear from animals.

Lesson Five: Auditory Information

Figure 20: Tango, the poo-eating guru, AKA Poo-ru

Before I spoke with an eight-month-old Boston Terrier named Tango, his human companion, Jenn, had emailed me with a variety of concerns, ranging from Tango's poop-eating tendency to his insistence on walking through the house at night and waking her in the middle of the night. Here's what Tango had to say about his nighttime ramblings:

"I'm a master healer, and Jenn is my student. I've been a healer before, in many different lifetimes. I'm teaching her things that are more important than sleep. When I wake her up in the night, she needs to pay attention to me. She needs to sit up and open her mind to my teachings. I will download the information, so she doesn't have to try to understand it. But she has to be awake, because her brain has to be running on a frequency of awareness."

I think I know a fair amount about energy healing and metaphysical stuff, but this little dog was telling me things I had never before imagined—things about poo-eating puppies being spiritual gurus, about crystal healing properties and plugging into the grid of the universe. I typed as fast as I could to keep up.

When I read through the transcript to correct any typos I'd made in my rush to receive all the information, I knew that I would be biting my nails from the time I hit "send" until the time I heard back from Jenn.

What would she think when I told her that her poop-eating puppy was a spiritual guru? Would she think I was crazy when I relayed the information (in downloadable, printable form, no less) about invisible crystal-like formations and energy healing and plugging into the grid of the universe?

You might think that sending this sort of "out there" information to a client you don't know might feel a little (or a lot) like going out on a limb.

And, you'd be right.

But as I've said before, people usually draw to them the animals they need, and Jenn was, in fact, very knowledgeable about the healing properties of gemstones. She understood everything Tango had to say, even if I didn't.

LESSON FIVE HIGHLIGHTS

🐾 Accurate auditory information, like accurate visual information, is often surprising, something you didn't expect.

🐾 Accurate auditory information will often come through in a way that sounds like the sort of conversation you're used to having with humans.

🐾 Auditory information that isn't easy to obtain may still be right.

🐾 You know you're getting accurate verbal information when the other animals in the household give corroborating testimony. Or, they may disagree, but provide a reason.

🐾 When auditory information is paired with visual information, it is easier to be confident that both are correct.

🐾 It's a pretty good indication that you're getting accurate verbal information when an animal gives an opinion that opens a window into the animal's worldview.

🐾 it's also a pretty good indication that you're getting good verbal information when an animal tells you something that

Lesson Five: Auditory Information

challenges your worldview or gives you fresh—or even astonishing—insight into the workings of the universe.

LESSON FIVE TASKS

1. Meditate daily.

2. Continue practicing daily telepathic conversations with different animals, getting validation from the animal's human whenever possible, and making notes. Remember that your own animal companions are eager to help, too.

3. Using your highlighter pens, underline correct info in green, maybe-or-partially-correct info in yellow. Flag seemingly-incorrect information with a red line in the margin (don't strike through the words).

4. Write about your experiences so far, and choose a few of these questions to answer. You can always come back to the rest later.

    a. Did you receive any surprising auditory information?

    b. Did the auditory information flow easily, or was it more like "pulling teeth?"

    c. Did you notice any accents or speech patterns that revealed an animal's personality?

Lesson Five: Auditory Information

    d. Did you receive any information that revealed an animal's opinion or worldview?

    e. Did any of the information challenge your beliefs or reveal insights about the workings of the universe?

    f. Did you receive any information that was corroborated—or challenged—by other animal family members?

    g. Have you noticed any patterns of ease or blockage in the way you receive information? When you feel it's easy, can you pinpoint what you're doing right? When you're feeling blocked, can you figure out why? Is it you? Is it them? Is it the situation?

    h. Have you noticed any self-judgment or condemnation as you write about your experiences? Can you think back and remember when any negative belief systems about yourself were planted?

5. You're almost halfway through the course now! Has any resistance come up? Have you been tempted to stop practicing on some days? This sometimes happens right before a breakthrough; the part of you that thinks new things are scary will try to put the brakes on what feels like

uncontrolled forward momentum. If this happens, and powering-through isn't working, give yourself an off-day from practicing, and instead take yourself out into nature. Go for a hike through the forest, sit on a beach, or just hang out in your own back yard with your animal companions.

6. Dig through some old childhood photos and find a few that have animals in them. When you need a new animal to communicate with during practice time, check in with your childhood animal companions. Animal communication is a spirit-to-spirit connection, so it isn't necessary for the animal to be alive. Your animal friends who have passed on may have wonderful advice to give you.

LESSON SIX: Feeling Information

In this lesson, I will give specific examples of what it is like to receive feeling information telepathically, and summarize key points to help you remember them. By the end of this lesson, you will have a firm grasp of the many ways feeling information can be experienced.

Figure 21: *Our cat Max feels more like a dog than a cat. His consciousness state is that of a big dog. Large and in-charge, he trains puppies to respect cats. If he likes being a dog so much, why is he a cat? Because cats are able and allowed to do things that dogs can't, including lying on top of the papers on my desk when I'm trying to work.*

How to Tell You Are Getting Accurate Feeling Information

Feeling information can be experienced as a physical sensation, emotion, energy level, or consciousness state. This can feel either subtle or overwhelming. People who have difficulty keeping good boundaries are especially vulnerable to absorbing the feelings of others. Ironically, learning how to receive feeling information telepathically can teach you how not-to-be a psychic sponge.

🐾 **When you connect in with an animal and get an immediate sense of their consciousness state, it is a good indication that you are on track.**

Consciousness state is a big-sounding term that means the animal's mindset, or way-of-being in the world. Max has the consciousness state of a big, calm dog. He is not afraid of dogs, and he allows new dogs or puppies who visit the farm to come close and check him out. If a dog gets too nosy, Max isn't afraid to pop them on the nose, but he knows better than to run from them and inadvertently activate their prey drive.

A dog who competes in agility trials might have the consciousness of a champion, and one would hope so, because if he has the consciousness of a timid mouse, he won't have much fun doing agility.

A cat who likes to lie around and be admired might have the consciousness of a Diva or a princess. A cat who rules the household and terrorizes the dogs might have the consciousness of a conquerer. I've met a few small dogs who have the consciousness of an army general or even Napoleon.

An old horse might have the consciousness state of a Buddha, and his energy level would correspond to his consciousness state. A Buddha's energy might be quiet, wise, content. Not motivated to do much, but happy just to BE.

🐾 **Feeling information, whether it's of the physical or emotional variety, can be much more subtle than visual or auditory information. It might be difficult to tell whether the feeling is yours or the animal's.**

When I connected with a dog named, Skipper, I got a feeling of nervousness and anxiety, but it was very subtle. I wasn't sure whether it was my own mental state (always a possiblity) so I put both feet flat on the floor, took a few deep breaths, and made sure I was centered and grounded.

The faint feeling of nervousness remained, and I was sure now that it wasn't me. But it could easily have been caused by a person Skipper didn't know (me!) popping into his head. So I introduced myself, explained what I was doing, and started the conversation with small talk.

I asked Skipper what he liked about being a dog. He showed me pictures of digging and rolling in the dirt and leaves. He said that he liked being outside, under the trees. He liked barking at the world, an activity which to him felt like singing. He said that he loved the squirrels, and that they loved him and his singing. He was happy to share the back yard with the squirrels, and they all enjoyed playing chase together. The squirrels knew he had no intent to harm.

After a bit more casual conversation, Skipper had relaxed, and the slight feeling of nervousness disappeared.

> If you aren't sure whether the feelings you are experiencing belong to you or the animal, take a break from the communication, put your feet on the floor, take a few deep breaths, and check in with yourself. Being centered in your own body and grounded in your environment will help you to separate your feelings from the animal's.

Feeling information can come as a feeling of sadness, grief and abandonment that brings tears to your eyes and lingers long after you've finished the communication. It can come as a knot in your stomach that makes you want to double over.

It can also come as a sudden onset of any emotion, including fear.

Lesson Six: Feeling Information

This happened to me when I spoke with a nine-year-old Labradoodle named Lola, who had developed severe storm phobia and separation anxiety. Lola had, several times, gotten herself shut up in the bathroom when the humans weren't at home, and she destroyed the door frame trying to get out.

When I first connected with Lola, an immediate feeling of being watched made me look over my shoulder to make sure no one was looking in through my office window. I knew the fear was Lola's, not mine, because I feel safe at home. I asked Lola why she had suddenly become afraid of storms.

"I don't know," she said. "I'm nervous all the time now, but storms make it worse."

Lola used the word nervous, but already I knew that her feeling was one of fear, because I could feel it myself. I asked, "Do you know what is making you nervous?"

"I don't know," she said. "I'm sorry. I feel bad. I did wrong. I'm in trouble."

I assured Lola that she wasn't in trouble; that her human family only wanted to help her feel better. Relieved that she wasn't in trouble, Lola let me know that her feeling of being unsafe in her home was a new feeling. So, something recently had changed in the home.

Again, I had the feeling, myself, of being targeted by some unseen force, the irrational worry of monsters lurking in every corner. Lola showed me images of herself hiding in the bathroom to escape something she felt was chasing her, then having the door slammed shut, trapping her inside. She couldn't tell me who, or what, was terrorizing her, or where the unseen force was coming from.

Remember, fear can block communication. It can block the animal's ability to think rationally and reason-out what is going on.

> The animal can't always fill in every blank, so sometimes you will have to do some detective work. Just be sure that you are always clear about which information is coming from the animal, and which information is coming from your ability to observe the situation and the environment.

I believed that something in the environment must be to blame. So I made a house call to the client's home in a neighborhood of estate-sized properties, to see if I could pick up anything from the environment.

I couldn't; there was nothing in Lola's home or her persons' behavior that led me down any particular path of inquiry. But in my conversation with Lola's humans, I learned that the year before, the next door neighbor had died under mysterious circumstances. Since then, they'd noticed strange things like lights coming on in the middle of the night. It didn't take a huge

Lesson Six: Feeling Information

leap of imagination to deduce that the neighbor's ghost had been terrorizing Lola.

And here's your reminder: It's important to always clear, ground, and protect yourself before every session. Because you may encounter something like this when you least expect it.

Clearing yourself will insure that your own body-mind-spirit is neutral, so you won't be projecting some latent pain or emotion you're carrying unconsciously. Grounding yourself will insure that you're fully present, ready and able to receive. Protecting yourself will insure that you don't inadvertently absorb anyone else's emotional or physical issues.

Ghost-busting is beyond the scope of this book, and if you're not trained to deal with spirits and entities, please don't try to remove them. Get help or refer your client to someone with experience (I've included some resources on my website, www.HearThemSpeak.com). I have been trained to help spirits and entities to move on to their next right place, and even so, I have referred clients out in situations that seemed too hot for me to handle.

In this case, I gave the neighbor's spirit the energy healing needed to release emotional turmoil, and I made sure that Archangel Michael was there to shepherd the liberated spirit safely to the light.

It was interesting to watch the dogs in the household while I did the session. When I first liberated the man's spirit from its earthbound state, one of the dogs started growling at one particular spot in the room. When Archangel Michael took the spirit to the light, the dog who'd been so terrorized came up to me, put her head in my lap, and gave a great sigh of relief.

🐾 Feeling information can help to locate physical problems.

You can ask an animal to send feeling information when there is a question about physical matters. Some good questions are, "Can you show me how you feel physically?" or "Does your body hurt or feel discomfort anywhere? Can you show me where?"

After you've asked a physical "feeling" question, you can open to the information by closing your eyes and imagining that you can slip inside the animal's body. If you're communicating with a dog, you'll imagine your body morphing into a dog's body. Then you'll do a body scan, just as you'd do for yourself if you wanted to pinpoint some subtle feeling of pain or discomfort. You'll see where your attention wants to stick. It can come as an actual feeling, or as a heightened awareness of one particular part of the body.

Lesson Six: Feeling Information

Figure 22: *Our cat Ulrich (Ulrich von Lickshimself) has a hitch in his get-along. His hips are off-kilter from an old injury. Connect with Ulrich telepathically and see whether your attention wants to stick in one particular area of his spine. Is one area hazy, dark, or shaded in your mind's eye when you look at this picture and ask to see where it hurts?*

I worked with a cat who'd been acting out by attacking other cats in the household. I asked him to show me whether anything was causing him to feel out of sorts, and I had a sensation of my back teeth being "heavy" as if there was food stuck there. I even got up and brushed my teeth in case the problem was mine, but the feeling persisted for the duration of the session.

I gave all this information to the cat's human, who took him to the vet the next day. Sure enough, the cat's back teeth had a lot of built-up calculus that needed cleaning. As soon as the discomfort that had made him so cranky was removed, he stopped being such a meanie.

For practice, it's fun to ask any animal you're communicating with if they'll allow you to inhabit their body for a moment and show you what it feels like to be them. (Remember, always ask permission first.) Another way to heighten this type of awareness is to guide yourself through a visual meditation in which you become one with an animal.

See yourself flying, a hawk gliding on a high thermal current, then plunging down to catch its prey in sharp talons. See yourself swimming, a tiny fish in a school of its kind, darting this way, then that, part of a community of shared consciousness. Chose any animal, become them in meditation, and experience what it's like to be them. It's a great way to hone your skill of inhabiting another creature's skin. It's fun, too!

Lesson Six: Feeling Information

🐾 Feeling information of the emotional variety often comes through uninvited.

Empathy for an animal's emotions comes naturally and easily to most people who are interested in animal communication. If you're reading this book, you're probably already good at feeling an animal's emotions. But like anything else, even the reception of emotions can be blocked or projected. It's always important to be clear and empty of your own agendas and opinions before you initiate communication with an animal. If an animal sends feeling information unasked, check in with your own body, your own emotions, to make sure you're not projecting your own opinions into the situation.

> You know you're getting accurate feeling information when the feeling or emotion is a distinct change from how you were feeling before you received the information.

Figure 23: *This is our cat, Princess Grace. A good question to ask a cat is "Can you show me what it feels like to purr?"*

Lesson Six: Feeling Information

I have been owned by many cats throughout my life. Even after I started communicating professionally, it never occurred to me to ask a cat what it felt like to purr. Then, one day, a half-wild stray cat gave me that gift.

I think maybe he was the one to do it because it was a surprise to him, too. He was a spooky little thing; we'd heard him meowing in the woods near the house for days before we saw him. I fed him far from the house so he would feel safe from humans, dogs, and other cats while eating. Every day, I moved his bowl of kibble a little closer to the house.

Finally, after about two weeks, we could see him, a three-month-old yellow tabby. We named him Spook, because he was like a little ghost—or spy—lurking the perimeter, trying to be invisible. It took several more weeks for me to lure him onto the porch so he could eat with the other cats. It took even longer before I could touch, and then pet him.

My morning routine—actually my routine most of the time—is fairly hectic. I'm usually running from one thing to the next the moment my feet hit the floor, because I know that by bedtime, I'll be rushing to fit one more thing from the long to-do list into my schedule.

I'll admit that except when I'm communicating, writing, or making art, I'm not always grounded. Scooping cat food into the bowls on the cats' feeding station is just one more click of the hamster wheel I'm on. I'll pause long enough to pet each of the cats who leap onto the table, but it's for their benefit, not mine.

On one particular day, I was rushing through my routine, scooping food into the line of bowls, plop, plop, plop, and giving a quick stroke on the back of each cat who leapt up onto the table to start eating.

When I stroked Spook, even while he was wolfing down his food (eating as if each meal might be his last) he arched his back and started purring. I felt an immediate sense of joy, serenity, and expansiveness open in my chest, a not-so-subtle vibration that felt like a ball of sunshine swirling outward, filling my heart chakra, then my whole body. It was an incredible feeling, a bit like an orgasm but centered in the heart.

Spook seemed as surprised by his sudden desire for human touch as I was. When I petted Spook on this day, he stopped eating, turned around, and presented his arched back for me to pet again, all the while purring like a Harley.

While I petted him, the feeling of sunlight-in-the-chest projected directly from his heart chakra into mine. It slowed me down, changing my focused determination into an expansive appreciation for that moment's joy.

Lesson Six: Feeling Information

🐾 Feeling information can be experienced as a reaction in your body: a sudden chill, or even a yawn.

When I'm doing remote energy healing, I often experience the client's shift as a yawn. It's not unusual for me to be sitting in front of my computer, typing up a healing session and yawning so much that tears stream down my face!

Sometimes, feeling information comes as a wash of cold air through your body, or the fine hairs on your arms standing up.

I call this my "truth meter" going off. It often happens when a conversation with an animal has revealed a deep and meaningful truth, or when a huge shift has occurred during an energy healing session.

Figure 24: *I was connected telepathically to Ella at the moment she crossed the Rainbow Bridge. A wash of cold air swept through my body when she transcended her physical form and became pure spirit. Photo by Michael Loftis.*

Ella's Transition

As an animal communicator and energy healer, I am often invited to witness miracles. And yet, it's easy to doubt the power of energy healing and the truth of psychic abilities, even when you experience them daily. It's easy to doubt yourself. But every now and then, a telepathic conversation with an animal gives you a "cookie," a small, verifiable nugget of information to keep the doubt-monster at bay. And occasionally, you are reminded in a big way that you are connecting with Source Energy and working with other Beings of Light to participate in making miracles.

For several months, I had been sending energy healing to Ella, a beautiful and sweet Pomeranian belonging to a client and friend named Pat. Ella had a heart condition that should have limited her life to two years, but at six years of age, she was still spreading joy to her human and dog family. But Ella was getting tired. Her valiant heart was failing. Pat had used every means available to help Ella live a long and happy life, but now it was time to ease her transition from this world to the next.

Ella's time to transcend came when Pat was out of town and Ella was staying with Marcia, a friend who loved Ella and had cared for her many times when Pat had to travel. Marcia knew Ella was nearing the end of her life and having difficulty breathing. Marcia called me, and over the phone, I did a healing session that eased Ella's breathing and helped her to relax. We

Lesson Six: Feeling Information

weren't trying to prolong Ella's life, only to ease her passing. We both felt certain that Ella wouldn't last the night. But she did.

The next evening, Marcia called again. Ella's breathing had worsened, and she was suffering. But something was keeping her from letting go. Even though Pat had given permission for Ella to cross the rainbow bridge, Ella was clinging to life. She still hadn't given herself permission to relinquish her failed body and step into pure spirit.

Over the phone, while Marcia held her, I helped Ella release any promises or pacts that were keeping her tied to her body and the earth. Then, when the session was complete, I closed my eyes and summoned the angels. I imagined them forming a circle around Ella while one angel leaned over her body and lifted her spirit out. Carrying her in his arms, he flew her over the Rainbow Bridge to the group of spirit dogs waiting on the other side, dogs Ella had known in this life and in others.

When I envisioned the angel lifting Ella's spirit from her body, I heard Marcia gasp. When I saw the angel fly Ella over the Rainbow Bridge toward her companions, I felt a cold wash of air run through my body. And Marcia said, "Oh! She's gone!"

Being present for death is as sacred as being present for birth, and in a way, it's the same thing, because death to the body is a rebirth of spirit. I was honored to be present for Ella's transition, even though it was over-the-phone and not in-person. But where my body was in that moment didn't matter, because I was there in the most real way possible. I was there in spirit, calling in the angels and watching them take Ella over the bridge to her new life.

Is this evidence that the Rainbow Bridge and angels and spirit animals are real? Even if I hadn't believed before, this experience would have convinced me because I felt the connection with Ella and her transition so deeply.

But you don't have to believe just because I do, and it isn't necessary for you to have any particular spiritual beliefs in order to be a great animal communicator. Remember, animals can and do communicate non-literal images to convey their intended meaning. Whether your mind wants to interpret the experience as literal fact or a figurative representation of something else doesn't matter, as long as you convey it accurately to the animal's human.

- **Feeling information may be experienced as a physical sensation inside your body or through your hands. Or, it can be even more subtle than that: a feeling that one part of the animal's body doesn't feel connected to the rest.**

When you're working with an animal in-person, and you know that it is safe to touch the animal or hover your hands slightly above his body, the proximity might cause your hands to feel warm, or tingly, or cold.

Even working remotely, you may feel the sensation in your body. Or, you might not physically feel anything, but your

Lesson Six: Feeling Information

attention may be drawn to a part of the animal's body that is warmer or colder or somehow different than the rest.

Often, these areas that feel different can indicate stuck, stagnant energy caused by a physical, mental, emotional, or spiritual issue—or a combination of these.

A tingling sensation might be an indication of a nerve problem. A cold sensation might indicate a lack of circulation, or it could be a spiritual disconnection caused by emotional trauma. You won't know until you ask.

It's not uncommon for an animal to become disconnected from a part of its body that still holds trauma from previous abuse. Cats and dogs sometimes chase their tails for fun, but it can also happen because they don't recognize the back half of their body as a part of themselves. There's a video on YouTube of a dog whose back leg keeps reaching for the bone he is guarding, and whenever his foot gets close to the bone, he turns and attacks his own foot, snarling and snapping viciously. It's a funny video until you realize that it shows a very disturbed little dog who doesn't fully inhabit his body.

Past trauma that is still embedded in the body can cause an animal to present a Jekyll and Hyde personality that is sweet and cuddly one moment, and a demonic fury the next. In a situation like this, animal communication can determine the source of the problem, and energy healing can help to relieve, reduce, or eliminate it.

People want—and often expect—a quick fix, but some problems have many layers and facets to be dismantled before an unhealthy pattern can be collapsed. Especially in situations involving abuse, an animal may not tell you everything there is to tell in the first session. Sometimes, it will take many sessions before they will trust you enough to reveal the core issue. And sometimes, they have suppressed memories of trauma that may not surface immediately or at all.

- **You know you're getting accurate feeling information when it's paired with other modes of communication, such as visual or auditory.**

Because feeling information is easily confused with your own emotions or body sensations, it is good to get verification by asking the animal to confirm your feelings in words or images: "I'm feeling ____. Is that how you feel? Can you show me what happened?"

I once spoke with a gray and white tabby named Toby. I asked Toby what he liked about being a cat. His energy came through right away, high-strung, happy, like a kitten filled with excitement at the joy of exploring new things. The *feeling* of his energy was paired with *words*.

"I like sitting up high, looking down on everything below me. I was a hawk in a previous lifetime and I liked that even better, but I thought I'd try being closer to the ground this time. I enjoy the

Lesson Six: Feeling Information

power and grace of my feline body. I like to hide and pounce and play hunting games." He also sent a *visual* image of sitting on a second-story windowsill looking out onto the branches of a big oak tree.

When it comes to self-verification, this communication yielded a trifecta of feeling, auditory, and visual. Then, when I spoke with one of Toby's humans, I was informed that he does like to look out the second-story window onto a large oak tree.

There are two levels of verification. First, it's important to self-verify as information comes in. Does it feel right? Does the information come in more than one mode? Did it flow, or was I reaching? Was I neutral, or was I trying to accomplish something? Even the desire to help an animal, or the need to reassure an animal's human companion, can create a subconscious agenda that blocks true communication.

The second level of verification lies in relaying everything you received, as faithfully as possible, to the animal's human companion. If they have questions, or if anything you received seems murky or unsubstantiated, go back in and communicate with the animal again. Ask more questions, dig deeper. See if you can find what you missed, or understand where you may have misinterpreted something. It's helpful to do this second check-in with the animal while you have the human companion on the phone, so you can have a three-way conversation between yourself, the animal, and the animal's human.

🐾 You are most effective as a communicator when you remain neutral.

Surgeons must be ruthless. They must be willing to do something that hurts in the short term, in order to effect beneficial change in the long term. They can't afford to tell a patient what he'd like to hear, when what that patient really needs is the truth.

> When we're talking about feeling information, let's not forget that we, as animal communicators, have feelings we must set aside in order to become clear channels of communication.

One important addition to the subject of feeling information is this question that you should ask yourself at regular intervals: *Have I inadvertently inserted my own feelings into this communication?*

The desire to help, the need to reassure, the hope of not hurting anyone's feelings, can trip up even a seasoned professional animal communicator.

Nice people make mistakes with their animals. Nice, well-meaning people do lasting harm without meaning to. We must make sure that in our hurry to reassure these nice people, we don't miss the opportunity of a teachable moment.

Lesson Six: Feeling Information

People usually come to animal communicators when their animals are acting out. Often, the animals are only responding to something their humans are doing, and if the humans don't know what they are doing wrong, they can't correct their behavior. We need to set our own feelings aside and meet each person at their current level of understanding. Then we can gently guide them up that spiral hill to the next level.

Animal communicators are, quite often, walking a tightrope. Like cops, and social workers, and therapists, animal communicators can assist in the education of people and the transformation of situations. But to do that, we should take in what's happening without judgement then lead someone, safely and compassionately, to their own transformative moment.

> When you are deciding what to say—and what not to say—to an animal's human, consider this sage advice of unknown origin: Is it true? Is it kind? Is it necessary?

Is it true? How sure are you of the information you have received? Have you self-verified by asking the animal to tell you or show you the information in a different way? That may not matter in questions of small importance. But when something really matters, take the time to be as sure as possible that you have received a clear answer from the animal, one that is not colored by your own opinions or agendas.

Is it kind? This question can have more than one answer. It may be hurtful for a person to hear something they don't want to hear. But if it might ultimately be more harmful for them or someone else if they don't hear it, you have to find a way.

Is it necessary? A good friend of mine is famous (to me, anyway) for saying, "You don't have to tell everything you know."

I have never encountered an animal who said something unkind in an effort to hurt their human's feelings. I have, however, had animals give me information that could conceivably make their person unhappy if they knew.

For example, a client who uses a wheelchair accidentally ran over her tiny puppy and broke its leg, though she didn't realize it at the time because it happened so quickly that the puppy didn't yelp. When she noticed the little dog limping, she thought that perhaps something in the yard had fallen on the puppy's leg

Lesson Six: Feeling Information

during a potty break outdoors. She would have felt horrible if she'd known the truth. Giving her the knowledge of what really happened wouldn't have helped the puppy, who now knew to stay out from under the chair's wheels. And, he had forgiven her the moment the accident happened.

Would the knowledge have helped some potential future puppy if it caused my client to be more careful in the future? Maybe. My decision not to tell may impact some not-yet-born and maybe never-to-be-born puppy. But in weighing the concerns of a fictional puppy against the feelings of my client, I decided in favor of my client.

In my place, you might have made a different decision, and that's fine. The important thing is that you don't forget to ask those questions when you need to.

LESSON SIX HIGHLIGHTS

🐾 Feeling information can be experienced as a physical sensation, emotion, energy level, or consciousness state.

🐾 When you connect in with an animal and get an immediate sense of their consciousness state, it is a good indication that you are on track.

🐾 Feeling information, whether it's of the physical or emotional variety, can be much more subtle than visual or auditory information. It might be difficult to tell whether the feeling is yours or the animal's.

🐾 If you aren't sure whether the feelings you are experiencing belong to you or the animal, take a break from the communication, put your feet on the floor, take a few deep breaths, and check in with yourself. Being centered in your own body and grounded in your environment will help you to separate your feelings from the animal's.

🐾 Be clear with yourself and the animal's human about which information is coming from the animal, and which information is coming from your ability to observe the situation and the environment.

Lesson Six: Feeling Information

🐾 Feeling information can help to locate physical problems.

🐾 Feeling information of the emotional variety often comes through uninvited.

🐾 You know you're getting accurate feeling information when the feeling or emotion is a distinct change from how you were feeling before you received the information.

🐾 Feeling information can be experienced as a reaction in your body, such as a sudden chill or a yawn. It can also be experienced as a physical sensation inside your body or through your hands. Or, it can be even more subtle than that: a feeling that one part of the animal's body doesn't feel connected to the rest.

🐾 You know you're getting accurate feeling information when it's paired with other modes of communication, such as visual or auditory.

🐾 You are most effective as a communicator when you can remain neutral and set aside your own feelings in order to become a clear channel of communication.

🐾 When you are deciding what to say—and what not to say—ask yourself: Is it true? Is it kind? Is it necessary?

Hear Them Speak

LESSON SIX TASKS

Choose a few of the following questions to answer in your animal communication notebook. Even when the questions could be answered in a one-word or one-sentence answer, don't cheat yourself. You're spending a lot of time and energy on this, and yet it is human nature to try to skip the hard stuff and still get the same result.

Dig deep, mine your inner landscape, and work hard to excavate your blocks and use them to build a firm foundation for this incredible skill you are building. Writing about your experiences—good, bad, indifferent, or undefinable—will help you to categorize and remember information and come up with new insights you might not have considered otherwise.

1. This was a huge lesson, I know. So before you do anything else, pat yourself on the back for getting through it. Feeling information can be the most subtle, the most overwhelming, and the most-often experienced mode of reception. Usually, it is paired with other modes, so it has a way of fading into the background and yet coloring everything else we receive. You deserve a big reward for tucking this lesson under your belt. Do something nice for yourself in the coming week.

2. This week, did you experience any feeling information that came through in a physical way inside your body or through

Lesson Six: Feeling Information

your hands? How did it feel? Was it subtle, or powerful? Did you scan your own body to make sure the feeling was coming from the animal and not from yourself?

3. Did you experience any feeling information as an emotion, energy level, or consciousness state? When did it happen? Was it at the beginning, middle, or end of the communication session? How did it feel? Subtle? Powerful? Did you ask for the information, or did it appear on its own?

4. Did your "truth meter" go off with a feeling of goosebumps, hair standing on-end, or a wash of cold air?

5. Did you experience any feeling information, physical or emotional, that was a distinct change from the way you were feeling before the communication? Did you scan your own body to make sure the feeling wasn't yours? Why or why not?

6. Did you receive feeling information along with visual, auditory, or other modes of information? Which was stronger? Did you feel more validated when the information came in more than one way? Was it automatic, or did you ask the animal to send the information in another way?

7. Have you had to dig deeper with any communications after speaking with the animal's human? Why do you think that was? Did you miss something? Misinterpret something? Were you able to discover more of the animal's message by working as a team with the animal and their human?

8. Have you noticed any insecurities rising up to block you? Can you figure out what triggered them? How did you overcome the block? Or is it still there? What will you do if it happens again?

9. How are your family and friends responding to your new skills? Are you feeling the need to defend yourself, or are you the new celebrity in town? (Having to defend yourself doesn't mean you're bad, and being called a celebrity doesn't mean you're good. Both reactions are reflections of your own insecurities and grandiose illusions. It helps to remember that neither is real.)

LESSON SEVEN: Smell, Taste, and Knowing

In this lesson, I will give specific examples of what it looks and feels like to receive smell, taste, and knowing information telepathically, and summarize key points to help you remember them. By the end of this lesson, you will have a firm grasp of the many ways that smell, taste, and knowing information can be experienced.

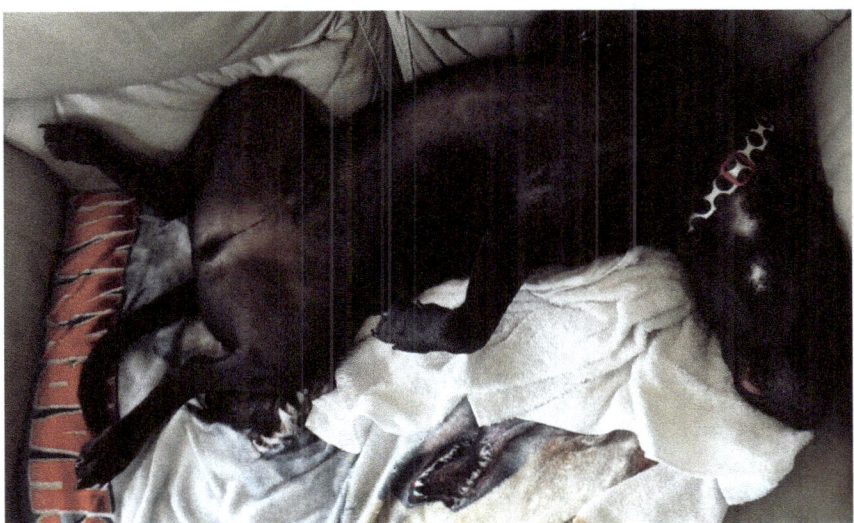

Figure 25: *If you asked Jed to tell you about his favorite place, he might send you a memory of the taste of salt water and the smell of ocean air. Here he is, passed out on the Sharknado towel after a long day of chasing balls on the beach.*

How to Tell You're Getting Accurate Smell or Taste Information

I will be combining the last three modes of reception into this one lesson because smell and taste occur less often than any of the other modes, so there is less ground to cover. After the last lesson on the BIG area of feeling information, this lesson will feel a lot like a downhill slide. And that's where you are now! Downhill slide, more than halfway through the course. Wheee!

Once we have covered these last three modes of reception, we will be done with the theory of how telepathic information is received, and we'll start busting through any blocks you may have been experiencing.

Buckle your seatbelt; we're heading downhill.

🐾 Smell and taste information can come as a real-time experience, or as a memory.

For me, smell comes through more often than taste, and neither happens as often as seeing, hearing, feeling, or knowing. Even when communicating about favorite flavors or foods, it usually seems easier to convey and receive that information in ways that are more conversational or visual than experiential.

But you may be different, and the animals you communicate with may be different. Communicators tend to draw to them the animals and people they are most capable of helping. So even

Lesson Seven: Smell, Taste, and Knowing

though smell and taste aren't dominant modes of communication for me, they may be for you. Be open to any information without judging how it shows up.

The enhanced senses of smell or taste can sometimes show physical or medical stuff. A sour taste in the mouth, a smell of decay or blood, can show that something, somewhere in the animal's body, has gone awry.

🐾 Smell and taste will often show up together, and sometimes you will be given additional information, such as texture.

Once when I was asked to help find a lost cat, he showed me a visual of the area where he was hiding. I also got the taste of dust and a feeling of grittiness in my mouth. It turned out that the cat was under a trailer near a construction site, where the ground had been scraped raw, and dirt was constantly blown around, filling the air.

Let me point out that I didn't feel grit between my teeth, or taste dust in my mouth. It was more a remembrance of that feeling, of being in a place where the wind kicked up dust or dirt so fine that it infiltrated everything, including my mouth. It's something we've all experienced at one point or another, right?

Be careful not to be so literal in your expectations that you fail to recognize the often-subtle ways information comes in. You might sometimes get an actual taste in your mouth. But don't expect it to happen that way every time. You are more likely to have a fleeting thought or memory of your own past that evokes a smell or taste.

How to Tell You Are Getting Accurate Knowing Information

🐾 **Information that comes as an immediate "knowing" feels like remembering a book you've read or a course you took in school. You have the holistic knowledge of an entire event, or even a lifetime, available to you in an instant.**

Knowing is often paired with visual information; you'll see a movie clip of a seminal moment or turning point; and you'll also know the background information that led to that moment.

Example: A woman wanted to know why her shelter-rescued dog often woke in the middle of the night and howled. When I connected with the dog, I saw an image, a short movie-clip of the dog, chained to the trailer hitch of a truck bumper, howling into the night.

That was the image. It came with deep feelings of sadness, fear, and loneliness.

I had an immediate knowing that the truck was parked far from any home or structure where people lived, and the dog was left to guard a workshop or scrap yard entrance. He may have had some company on most days, but he was left entirely alone at night. In all kinds of weather, he remained chained to that

Lesson Seven: Smell, Taste, and Knowing

truck in a lonely place with barren, mountainous terrain, with no light coming from anything but the moon. Desperate and afraid, he worried that the coyotes that dug at the bottom of the fence would come in and kill him. I could hear his howls, low and mournful, as he cried out for someone, anyone, to come and rescue him.

Knowing often comes in a way that can tear at your heart.

Knowing can be difficult to verify, unless the animal's person happens to know the animal's background; and even then, there may be gaps in the human's knowledge, including gaps they aren't aware of. Because of that, it won't always be possible to get verification by asking the animal's human. It could be that they weren't at home with their animals when something stressful happened. Or someone in charge of a situation may have lied to avoid potential consequences. Events may have been misunderstood. Or, the person may not know their animal companion very well.

One way to verify information that comes through as a global sense of knowing is to check whether other modes of info gleaned in that same session were verifiable.

The more you practice, and the better you get at knowing when you're hooked-in and when you're not, the more you will be able to self-verify.

By now, you are probably beginning to get a sense of when you're "on" and when you're a little off-center. When you are having an on-fire session in which everything is clicking and you can *feel* it, that's a good way to self-verify.

- 🐾 **If knowing information comes during a session in which the other answers you were seeing, hearing, or feeling resonated as being right, then you can be more confident in the information that came through as knowing.**

Lauren—one of my clients who later became a student—noticed a stray dog that had been hanging around a parking lot for several days. She sent me a picture of the dog who looked sad, resigned, and distrustful. Lauren inquired in the store, and was told that the dog had shown up the week before and wouldn't let anyone come near her.

The dog let me know that she was waiting for her people to come and find her. I asked how she'd come to be in the parking lot, and she showed a visual of herself falling out of a moving pickup truck. I felt the dog's emotions of guilt, fear, and betrayal. And, I noticed from the picture that she wasn't wearing a collar.

I asked the dog to show me how she'd fallen out of the truck, and I didn't get a clear picture. But of course, falling from a moving vehicle would have been a lightning-fast, traumatic event. And animals, just like people, sometimes block out memories that are too disturbing to recall without extreme emotional distress.

Lesson Seven: Smell, Taste, and Knowing

"I didn't mean to fall," she replied. "I get yelled at for getting up on the box, but I want to be inside the truck and I'm not allowed. I'm supposed to stand on my feet in the back, but I don't feel safe there."

My sense of knowing was screaming at me by this time: The dog had been shoved, or tossed, out of a moving truck, and then abandoned on the side of the road. Her feelings of guilt, fear, and betrayal, supported that sense of knowing.

The catch: Feeling and knowing are the hardest modes of reception to verify because they are most likely to be hijacked by your own opinions and biases. And because the dog wasn't remembering (or couldn't bear to remember) the event that caused her to fall from the truck, and she wouldn't speak ill of her human family, I didn't have any way to validate the information through visual or auditory information.

Figure 26: This stray dog had a hard time trusting people enough to get in the car with someone who wanted to help her. Animal communication and energy healing gave her the courage to allow herself to be rescued. Photo by Lauren Thomas.

So here's where it gets interesting. My sense of knowing, along with the dog's emotional reactions, contradicted what she was telling me!

Deciding which leads to follow can also be helped by asking those three questions I mentioned before:

Is it true? Maybe... I'm getting conflicting information.

Is it kind? It might be unkind to make the dog remember something that is so upsetting.

Is it necessary? Well, not really. Knowing whether the dog fell out by accident or was tossed out on purpose didn't really pertain to helping Lauren get the dog in the car—a priority because the dog needed food, shelter, and veterinary attention. And, bad weather was on its way, so we couldn't afford to waste time.

If the dog's person showed up to claim her, or if the dog turned out to have a microchip, the question of whether her abandonment was accidental or purposeful might be relevant. But right now, it wasn't. So I moved on with the conversation.

I asked the dog whether she would be willing to get into the car with Lauren.

Lesson Seven: Smell, Taste, and Knowing

"I'm not supposed to get inside the car," she replied. "That's bad. I don't get in the truck; I don't go in the house. I stay where I'm told to stay."

"I'm sure you're a very good girl," I assured her.

"I was bad," she replied. "I did wrong and that's why I fell out. That's why they won't come back and get me. I'm being punished. But I'll wait and be good and maybe they'll come back and get me. I won't do the bad thing again."

I was getting a very strong sense of knowing that this dog was like a kidnapping victim who knew that being tightly bonded to her tormentors was her only way of surviving. She was going to wait until her people came to get her, or until she died of malnutrition and exposure. I had to convince her, but I had to soft-pedal it so she could make the decision herself.

"If you want to wait there," I said, "you can. But at some point soon, the dog catcher may come and get you and take you to the dog pound, which feels a lot like doggie jail, even though they're trying to help." (I sent her a mental image of an animal shelter, because she didn't have a frame of reference.) "You could sleep inside a house instead of out in the rain. Wouldn't you like that?"

"I'm supposed to wait for my people. That's what they'd want me to do."

And yet, I had the strong feeling that they would never come to get her. So I had to keep pushing, but gently. Heavy thunderstorms were on the way, and the dog would be exposed and vulnerable. She may even be so frightened that she would run back out onto the nearby highway and get hit by a car.

"I think they'd want you to be safe," I said. "Lauren will put a sign in the store, so if your people come, they will know where to find you. That way, you can wait for your people in a safe place, with food and water and shelter."

> If you find a lost animal, put up a sign that says FOUND (dog, cat, or whatever) and your contact info. DO NOT DESCRIBE THE ANIMAL. Make anyone who calls give a description of the animal they have lost and answer any questions you deem necessary to make sure the animal will be safe if you return it to them. You can't kidnap a person's animal, but in cases of abuse or neglect, you may need to get the local authorities involved.

Lesson Seven: Smell, Taste, and Knowing

The happy ending to this story is that I did an energy healing session to help the dog release her fears along with any feeling of obligation that kept her from receiving help, and she got into the car with Lauren that evening, before the storm broke. No one ever responded to the FOUND DOG flyer in the store. The dog, whose name is Clover now, decided to stay with Lauren, where she will live happy-ever-after for the rest of her life.

(And stories like this are one reason why I love this job. Also, I can wear my pajamas all day long if I want to.)

🐾 **If the knowing comes through in a bowl-you-over way, with strong emotion or vivid visuals,** that's **a good indication** you're **on the right track.**

Judy Behrens, the owner of Panther Ridge, a big cat conservation center, asked me to connect with her jaguar, Bella, who hadn't eaten in three days. Bella had lost weight, and Judy was worried. I asked Judy to email me a photo of Bella, and when Bella's photo popped up onto my big computer screen, her longing and despair went straight to my heart.

Figure 27: *Bella, before animal communication helped her wishes to be understood. Photo by Anne-Laure Michelis.*

Bella's intense, far-gazing stare into the world outside her enclosure was something anyone looking at this photo could observe. But my sense of knowing told me that Bella's feelings had gone past—far past— longing into desperation.

Knowing is the most difficult mode of reception to verify, because it feels a lot like it could be your own thoughts and opinions. That's why it's important to verify your knowing with other modes of reception, and luckily, most of the time, knowing

Lesson Seven: Smell, Taste, and Knowing

will come along with words, visuals, feelings, smell, or taste, to help you self-verify.

My sense of knowing told me that Bella was so desperate to get out of her enclosure, she could think of nothing else, not even food. The words I heard her shout in my head were *out, out, out*!

With visual images, Bella showed me that her enclosure was large and clean, lush with vegetation and filled with hiding spots and places to climb. The visual came along with a *feeling* sense that Bella was loved and cared-for. When I asked what she liked to do for fun, she showed me that special toys and treats and activities were often provided for her amusement.

But she still wanted *out*, and nothing else would make her happy. Bored with her own space, she decided that the grass would be greener in another cat's domain. Her curiosity and longing had escalated to the point that getting *out* was all she could think of, and she didn't care whether she got out alive or dead.

I didn't know Judy, so this wasn't the sort of information I wanted to email in a transcript, as I usually would. I knew it would be too upsetting. So I called Judy instead, and after I delicately broached the subject, Judy and I brainstormed possibilities. Judy decided that she could let Bella spend a little time each week in another cat's enclosure while he stayed somewhere else. But the enclosure would have to be jaguar-proofed first. Judy said that the process would take about two weeks, and she promised to do it.

I connected with Bella and let her know the deal we had made. Judy would prepare the other cat's enclosure so Bella could spend several hours each week exploring the scents and textures of a new and exciting area. In return, Bella would have to 1) start eating again right away so she'd have the strength to enjoy her enrichment time, and 2) promise that she would willingly go into a transport cage when it was time to travel between enclosures.

In this case, my sense of knowing was supported by strong visuals, feeling, and auditory information. But when the visual and auditory information is sketchy or the conclusion can be easily passed-off as simple observation, you may have to take it on faith that your sense of knowing is correct—at least until a change in the animal's behavior provides verification.

The proof, as they say, is in the pudding. In Bella's case, the promise of a two-weeks-into-the-future excursion into a different enclosure caused a definite and immediate change in behavior: Bella ate a hearty meal that night, and when the time came, she kept her promise about transferring between enclosures with no fuss.

Using simple observation, it's easy to see from Bella's before and after pictures what a difference a little extra enrichment time made!

Lesson Seven: Smell, Taste, and Knowing

Figure 28: *Bella, enjoying her excursion into a different enclosure after she was able to tell us what she wanted. See how happy and relaxed she looks? Photo by Anne-Laure Michelis.*

One Last Caution about Knowing

I've read books on telepathic or psychic abilities that suggest you can rely on the first thing that pops into your head as accurate information. I disagree. Sometimes, your rational, left-brain will go into figure-it-out mode before you've achieved a deep connection with the animal. So, I'm apt to distrust the first thing that pops up, especially when it comes as knowing. Your opinions or suppositions can masquerade as knowing if you're not careful.

If you get a big hit of knowing information before you've deliberately connected with the animal, set it aside for a moment, take a few deep breaths, and do your routine of centering, grounding, protecting, and connecting. Then, ask the animal whether the information that came through was correct.

Lesson Seven: Smell, Taste, and Knowing

LESSON SEVEN HIGHLIGHTS

🐾 Communicators tend to draw to them the animals and people they are most capable of helping.

🐾 Smell and taste information can come as a real-time experience, or as a memory. Smell and taste will often show up together, and sometimes you will be given additional information, such as texture.

🐾 Information can also come as an immediate "knowing." This feels like remembering a book you've read or a course you took in school. Knowing can give you the holistic knowledge of an entire event, or even a lifetime, in an instant.

🐾 If knowing information comes during a session in which the other answers you were seeing, hearing, or feeling resonated as being right, then you can be more confident in the information that came through as knowing.

🐾 If the knowing comes through in a bowl-you-over way, with strong emotion or vivid visuals, that's a good indication you're on the right track.

🐾 Your opinions or suppositions can masquerade as knowing, especially if it is the first thing that "pops" into your mind.

LESSON SEVEN TASKS

By this point, I hope it goes without saying that you're practicing your communication skills with a different animal helper each day, and meditating for a few minutes every day.

Every day this week, choose one or two of the following questions to answer in your animal communication notebook. These questions are designed not only to help you remember your experiences, but to help you think more deeply about them and consider angles you might not have otherwise been aware of. Allow the questions to open a door for you to enter and explore more about the subject. Also, feel free to follow your own intuition into new and different areas I didn't include.

Tasks Regarding Smell and/or Taste Information:

1. Write about any smell or taste information you received.

2. Did you experience an actual smell or taste, or just the memory of it?

3. Were any emotions associated with those smells or tastes? Could the emotions have been a part of the information the animal was sending to you?

Lesson Seven: Smell, Taste, and Knowing

Tasks Regarding Information Received as Knowing:

1. Have you received knowing information that came all on its own, with no other modes of receiving along with it? If so, how confident (or not) did you feel about that information, and why?

2. Thinking about your opinions of how animals and humans should coexist in this world, could your sense of knowing have been bolstered by your own preconceived notions? Did your sense of knowing agree, or disagree, with your privately held opinions?

3. Have you received knowing information that was paired with other modes of receiving? If so, how confident (or not) did you feel, and why?

4. Did the sense of knowing come before the other senses? Or at the same time? Or only after you'd given it some thought? Which do you think would be more reliable?

5. How reliable does the information feel? Does circumstantial information support your knowing, or is it just a convenient foundation for a fiction you're creating in your imagination? It is easy to mistake opinion for knowing. Ask yourself some hard questions, and whenever possible, verify.

6. Have you received knowing information that was contradicted by other information you received, or by the animal's human companion?

7. Ironically, when knowing contradicts other available information or your opinion, that may be an indication that the knowing is correct. Write about any inconsistencies between your sense knowing and your opinion, or your sense of knowing and other available information.

8. Have you received knowing information that was subtle? Or knowing information that bowled you over? Which felt more reliable? Why? Is one better than the other?

9. Have you received knowing information that came through before you'd connected with the animal? Did you feel you could trust that information? Why or why not?

LESSON EIGHT: Common Blocks, Digging Deeper

In chapter two, I mentioned the most common blocks to clear communication. In this chapter, we are going to dig deeper into exploring those blocks and others. We will explore the ways in which they keep you from receiving clear telepathic information, and how you can avoid or get past them.

Figure 29: *Esmeralda is a good communicator, but if you're blocked, you won't understand what she wants you to know.*

In your practice so far, have you encountered any of these blocks?

- 🐾 strong emotions or opinions

- 🐾 external circumstances

- 🐾 the animal's human

- 🐾 higher-order needs

- 🐾 a too-busy mind

Have you felt unable to receive clear information but weren't sure what was blocking you? If so, no worries. We're about to blast through your blocks, those we've already covered plus a few extras, and even the ones you can't see.

Any Strong Emotion Can Block Communication

Let's do a quick run-through of some of the major emotions that can block communication, and briefly touch on ways in which these blocks appear. Afterward, we'll dig deeper into some of the biggies, and then I'll give you the tools to dismantle the ones that don't fall down the minute you recognize them.

Lesson Eight: Common Blocks, Digging Deeper

Knowing what each of these blocks looks like in action is sometimes all the ammunition you need to blast through them.

🐾 Worry, love, pity, frustration, anger, guilt, grief, fear: Any of these can block clear reception.

If you are worried that you will hear something upsetting, or even if you're just worried about your own problems, your mind may be churning on that worry. Even if you push the worry to the back of your mind, it can clog up your ability to receive clearly. It's like trying to concentrate on reading when the television is blaring in the next room. Your eyes are busy tracking the lines of print, but at some point you realize that you're not absorbing the information because your ears are tuned to the sound coming from another room.

Even love can block clear communication, because when you are so in love with your animal companion, you may be unwilling—consciously or subconsciously—to take the chance of hearing that they are unhappy or need something you can't provide. And you can't just decide to block one subject without muddying up the rest.

Feeling pity for an animal can keep you from feeling anything *but* pity. There may be a brave spirit inside that sad exterior, and if you're focused on appearances, you won't be able to connect deeply with the beautiful soul inside.

Frustration that you're not getting anything telepathically can keep you from getting anything telepathically! If you feel frustrated, check your body language. Are you leaning forward, hands clenched, forehead furrowed, trying hard to understand what the animal has to say? If so, your frustration has led to TRYING instead of ALLOWING. When you're leaning forward, it is likely that you are reaching for answers, which can then lead to making stuff up. If you are attempting to communicate and getting nowhere, check your posture. Make sure you are leaning back, relaxed, making space in your heart and mind for the information to flow.

Anger coming from you or the animal can block clear communication. If you are angry at your cat for peeing outside the litter box, your anger will be all the cat sees, and he won't be eager to communicate his reasons or listen when you try to explain why you don't love that behavior. If two dogs are fighting, they won't be listening to any telepathic message you try to send because they are focused on their anger to the exclusion of all else.

Guilt and grief often go hand in hand. These emotions can not only block communication, they can color everything—every relationship, every decision, every experience—in a person or animal's life. These emotions can expand until they take up all the room in the heart and mind of the person or animal, preventing them from communicating clearly.

Lesson Eight: Common Blocks, Digging Deeper

🐾 **Fear is probably the biggest emotional block to clear communication.**

An animal's human who is fearful of what they might learn can block your reception or discourage the animal from fully participating in a conversation. An animal who is fearful is also going to have a hard time communicating.

If you're afraid that you may receive upsetting information, your mind can play tricks on you and show you your worst fears instead of the truth. When that happens, your left brain (rational, making-things-up from worst-case scenarios) may kick in before you even connect with the animal. It's important to identify when your left brain is working overtime, and either ask another communicator to help, or wait until you feel clear.

Figure 30: *Fear of what I might learn kept me from even asking my missing goats and Lambert where they were. A foolish decision I soon came to regret. In the future, I'll try not to allow fear to keep me from even trying to communicate in an emotionally-charged situation.*

Lesson Eight: Common Blocks, Digging Deeper

What's the worst thing that could happen?

Blocking because of fear that you will learn something upsetting can happen to anyone; it even happened to me recently. In my case, I saw the worst-case scenario in my imagination every time I thought about connecting in, so I never did. I knew that my worst fears were coloring my ability to receive clear information, so I avoided the conversation altogether.

It happened when my husband and I were out of town for a week, and during this time, our four goats and one sheep disappeared. When my husband and I returned, we walked the fence line looking for a break, but everything was perfect. No gates were left open. There was, simply, no sign of the goats and sheep. It was as if the Mother Ship had beamed them up.

It was close to Labor Day, and we live way out in the country, so my worst-case scenario left brain told me that someone had stolen my goats to barbecue for the holiday. My worst-case scenario vision was a disturbing picture of my poor, friendly goats and Lambert the sheep hanging upside down from a big oak, throats slit, bleeding out. (One common trait artists, animal communicators and psychics share is a vivid imagination).

While my husband and I walked the fence line, calling and calling to no avail, my husband kept asking me why I didn't just connect-in and ask the goats and Lambert where they are?

I explained that I couldn't because I was too afraid of what I might find out. He just shook his head. Why decline to use your superpowers when it matters most? At the very least, I should have contacted one of my animal communicator friends and asked them to check in. But I didn't want to hear, even secondhand, that somebody in Baldwin County was dining on goat-and-lamb stew.

Finally, a couple of days after Labor Day, five days after the goat-and-sheep clan disappeared and all hope of finding them was lost, I decided that I had the strength and emotional neutrality to connect-in and find out what had happened. I resolved to do it that evening, after we'd run some errands, one of which required me to first get some boxes from the basement.

In the basement, instead of the boxes, I found… you guessed it… the goat-and-sheep collective. They were alive and well—if a little skinny. They had spent the week dancing on the tabletops, leaping from shelf to shelf, feasting off cardboard and paper and canvas and sheet rock, and drinking the buckets of water I used to reconstitute dry clay.

My 900 square-foot basement art studio, which had been full of clay sculptures and pottery and glazes—not to mention hundreds of glass bottles that I melt in the kiln to make wind chimes and other artsy-craftsy stuff—was now full of goats.

And goat shit.

And under all that goat shit was a melee of broken glass and pottery scattered over every square inch of that basement.

Circumstantial evidence revealed that someone who shall remain nameless (because nobody will fess up, though I know who it was) had gone through the basement door into the goat field to feed the goats instead of going around through the fence gates. That person then left the door ajar instead of closing it completely, so the goat collective felt free to come on in. And when they had knocked over enough things during their basement free-for-all, the debris of their destruction accumulated against the door and shut it firmly behind them, locking them in.

For five days. Five days to wreak havoc in my basement art studio.

Oh, if only I had gained the emotional neutrality I needed to connect-in on the first day or even the second day, I might have saved myself a whole lot of trouble.

It took over a month to clean that place. And the goat smell lingered for months.

The moral of the story: Consider trusting yourself and at least trying to connect, even in emotionally charged situations, sooner rather than later.

Projected scenes of worst-case scenarios from a lost animal's human (or yourself) can stand in the way of clear communication. So can projected hopes of best-possible outcomes. Lost animals are notoriously difficult to find for these reasons, and also because a lost animal may be too fearful to communicate well.

Think of a time when you were lost, driving in unfamiliar territory. Your rational brain goes on the fritz as it shuts off to fuel the reptilian brain's fight-or-flight response. You may be using a state-of-the-art guidance system, but its instructions can't get through to your rattled mind, which is busy spinning worst-case scenarios of death and destruction. Even though help is right in front of you, your brain isn't computing, so you take yet another wrong turn even deeper into the sketchy neighborhood.

- 🐾 **An animal who is afraid will also have a hard time communicating clearly. Higher-order needs of safety and sustenance may have to come first.**

Lost animals don't always remember where they've been, and they certainly don't know where they're going. Any information you get from them may be in out-of-order snippets that don't help you track their direction. They may be in panic mode, and if so, their brains may not correctly order and retrieve information.

If the lost animal is also injured, the problem is compounded.

Injured animals are often not well-anchored in their own body/mind as they try to distance themselves from the fear and pain they are feeling. They may be able to focus and communicate for a moment, then lose the connection as they go in and out of themselves.

Please remember, if you're working with an injured or fearful animal in-person, always approach them with caution—if at all—because they may bite. And if they do, it won't be their fault, it'll be yours. An animal who bites you may have to pay the ultimate price for your inattention, so please be mindful of your limitations—and theirs.

Lesson Eight: Common Blocks, Digging Deeper

We'll talk more in-depth about working with lost animals later. For now, I'm just introducing it as one way fears and emotions—ours, the animal's, or even the animal's human—can block us from receiving clear communication, and why higher-order needs must sometimes be fulfilled before the animal will want to communicate.

🐾 Higher-order needs apply to you, too.

Sometimes you may not be up to the task of communicating because of health issues or other circumstances that keep you from being fully present in the moment.

Even when you're working in front of your computer in a completely silent house, something as simple as a dive-bombing fly or whining mosquito can be a distraction.

An undone to-do list can be a distraction. My office window looks out onto the back yard. At this moment, there is a milkweed out there that I'm pretty sure is taller than I am. When the wind picks up, I can see the cotton-candy white seeds floating through the air, so that one plant this year will make fifty plants next year. And I may just have to stop typing right now, and go pull that weed. You may have to TCOB (take care of business) before you can communicate effectively.

You may be asked to find a lost pet, help with end-of-life decisions, or mediate in any number of stressful, sometimes even impossible, situations. You'll be asked to do these things when you're out to dinner, or when you're in bed with a cold.

Learn to say "NO" when you're not up to the task. Partly to protect yourself and your energy, but also to make sure that you're giving every client the best you have to offer. And just remember that those people who really don't want to know the truth are most likely to insist on your help when you're least able to give it. So for your own benefit as well as theirs, say no when you need to say no.

Then, there are other times when you don't need to say no, but you do need to take a moment, or a substantial break, to get yourself back together before you proceed. Many times, it just takes an ounce of self-awareness for you to know when you're losing focus and need to take care of yourself.

A lot of simple, fixable things can block communication. You haven't had a bathroom break in forever. You're too cold or too hot. You're too tired or hungry or thirsty. You didn't sleep well the night before. You have a headache. You just got a phone call or text that requires your attention. Your last communication was upsetting. Your last client argued with you because you told them something they didn't want to hear. I could go on forever, but you get my drift.

🐾 A too-busy mind is a block to communication.

Lesson Eight: Common Blocks, Digging Deeper

Do whatever it takes to calm your hamster-on-the-wheel that never stops turning. Teach that critter to take a nap so you can access the quiet space your mind needs for communication. Take a nap yourself if you need to. Meditate, get some energy healing, and manage your own resources of time and energy.

If you're having trouble connecting and the problem isn't the environment or the animal, take the time to center and ground yourself. It doesn't have to be a big production. You can do it in the space of a few deep breaths. Close your eyes, lean back in your chair, put your feet flat on the floor. Take a few slow, deep breaths. Check in with yourself. How are you feeling? Nervous? Anxious? Identify your emotional state then set the intention to release it.

Breathe in from the soles of your feet through the top of your head. On the in-breath, you're absorbing strength and calmness from Mother Earth. Breathe out from the top of your head through the soles of your feet. On the out-breath, you're releasing anything you don't need for Mother Earth to handle and transform. Visualize yourself emptying of everything that could get in the way of pure communication. Put down roots to anchor yourself to the core of the earth, and open your mind to the wisdom of Source energy.

When you feel that you've established a clear channel, try again.

Hear Them Speak

🐾 **If the animal's human is emotionally overwrought or worried about what you may find during a communication, they can actively (or subconsciously) block you from communicating with their animal companion.**

A woman approached me at a psychic fair and asked me to communicate with her deceased dog, even though she didn't have a photo of him. My only connection to the dog was his emotional bond to the woman. It's very possible to connect with an animal through a clear-headed human companion, even without a photo. I've done it many times. But this woman was fighting tears and clearly worried about what the dog might say.

I'm not particularly psychic with people, but it was easy to see that she was consumed with guilt over the dog's death. If she'd been willing to tell me anything of the situation, I might have been able to connect. Not necessarily because of any information she might have given me, but because of her willingness to participate.

She just sat in front of me like a human brick wall, arms crossed, closed-off. Lost in her despair, everything about her demeanor blocked me from giving answers she didn't want to hear to questions she couldn't bear to ask.

She shielded herself by testing me, asking for a connection and then withholding the only conduit that was available—herself. She didn't really want to know what her deceased animal had to

Lesson Eight: Common Blocks, Digging Deeper

say, because she had already judged and found herself guilty. She wanted absolution, but didn't think she deserved it, so she locked herself in a self-imposed purgatory.

If you haven't already, you will encounter people who will ask you for answers that they really don't want to hear. They will challenge you to connect and then actively (or passively) block you from making that connection.

This lady's motivation and modus operandi were straight-up easy to spot.

But some people are more subtle. You ask for a clear photo taken in daylight without a flash. They'll send you a blurry photo taken in daylight, following two of the instructions and leaving out the other. When you ask for a clearer image, they'll send one they took indoors with a flash, so the animal's eyes are transformed into glowing neon green (or red or white) alien orbs. You could go back and forth forever, but there will always be some reason they can't do exactly what you asked.

Were they absent from kindergarten when everyone else learned to follow directions?

No, they're just throwing out roadblocks.

Some people don't want to know what their animal thinks (or thought). They only want absolution and agreement. You will encounter people who only want to mess with you, challenge you, and tear you down. If you're not willing to tell them what they want to hear, they'll shop around for another communicator. Eventually they'll find someone who will take their money and spout whatever they want to hear. But you're not that sort of communicator. If you were, you wouldn't be reading this book.

You can communicate with an animal without a photo, and you can get to the heart of a problem without a list of questions and concerns. But you can work more effectively when the person enlisting your help is willing to work with you, as a team.

Your time is valuable. Don't waste it by proving yourself to people who don't want proof. Don't waste your time digging for the truth when they don't want to hear it. Don't let anyone make you doubt your abilities. If someone really wants your help, they'll do their part to meet you halfway.

But I should also mention here that not every person who sends you blurry photos is trying to block your ability to communicate with their animal. Some people are just technologically challenged. It's up to you to know the difference between someone who wants and needs your help, and someone who just wants to mess with you.

🐾 Another block to communication is your opinion.

Your opinion, your sense of how things should be, has no place in telepathic communication. You may have heard of the sage advice, "Judge not." Those two words go beyond the concept of judging your neighbor harshly. The art of not-judging anything is a key to serenity and objectivity. If we can see every event that we would normally judge as good or bad as just one step in each

Lesson Eight: Common Blocks, Digging Deeper

being's journey to their next right place, we can go beyond judgment into non-attachment to outcomes. And if we're not attached to any certain preference for the unfolding of a situation, we can be a clear channel to communication.

Simple? Yes. Easy? Not so much.

Figure 31: *People (and animals) often have strong opinions about how things should be. Should dogs sleep in the house? Jed thinks not. He wants to be outside patrolling all night long. But he isn't in charge around here, so he has to sleep inside. If you have an opinion about how animals should live, set it aside when you're communicating.*

Hear Them Speak

As I mentioned before, I have always believed that dogs should sleep inside the house with their people. Dogs are pack animals, and dogs who live disconnected from their human family often have anxiety about being shut out of the pack. This can result in problems like antisocial behavior (aggression, biting), destructive behavior (digging, chewing), anxious behavior (pacing, barking), and more. I'm still of that opinion, but I must set my opinion aside when I communicate with outside-only dogs, because my job as a communicator is to relay the animal's opinions, not my own.

I have spoken with many outside-only dogs who didn't want to come inside. Some find the interior of a house too confining. Others find humans too chaotic, too noisy, too busy.

Some dogs just prefer being outside. (And of course, we are talking about outside-only dogs who have access to a weatherproof shelter, ample food and clean water, and space to move around freely. Animal neglect is a crime, not a matter of opinion.)

The first time my belief system about dogs living outside was challenged was when I spoke with a small, indoor-only dog who was worried about her large, outdoor-only dog companion.

Tink (short for Tinkerbell), the indoor dog, was a Yorkie about two years old. Oliver, the outdoor dog, was an elderly Saint Bernard mix. The dogs' human companion, Angela, called me because Tink kept knocking over her bowl of kibble at feeding

Lesson Eight: Common Blocks, Digging Deeper

time, deliberately scattering the food everywhere instead of eating.

I talked with Tink (the Yorkie), and she let me know that she wanted Oliver to live inside, like everyone else in the family. It took a little time to get Tink to tell me in words what was going on. She wasn't used to communicating with humans except through physical interaction in which she mimed what she wanted to the best of her ability. She had reached the conclusion that humans were fairly stupid. She didn't believe she could talk directly with me, even when I told her she could.

I asked Oliver what he thought about living inside with the rest of the family. I had expected that he would say, "Yes! I want to live inside!" But instead, he showed me that he liked to communicate with the birds and the creatures that live outside. He and the local wildlife were close friends, and he would be sad to leave them for too long.

He said, "I would like to be more a part of the family inside, but I still want to spend most of my time outside." He showed a visual of himself standing still to get a bath because he knew that smelling clean would be an important requirement if he were to come inside.

He continued, "I know that Tink wants me to come inside because she worries about my health, but mostly she feels bad that I'm left out of the family circle. Sometimes I do think about coming inside, but nature and the other creatures that live outside are my family, too. I like lying out under the stars when the weather is nice. And I know that my presence outside the house protects my family and deters strangers from approaching the house."

Oliver considered himself a first-line-of-defense, and he valued his deep spiritual connection to the great outdoors. He was an articulate dog who nurtured his spiritual nature through solitude and his immersion in the natural world. He wouldn't have been as happy living indoors full time.

To make Tink happy, Angela agreed that Oliver would be allowed inside during feeding time and when cold or rainy weather made life outdoors uncomfortable.

In a follow-up phone call a couple of weeks later, Angela told me that Oliver was becoming more comfortable in the house, and though he preferred to spend most of his time outside, he often lounged inside for an hour or two after feeding time.

If I had used the opportunity of communication with Oliver to convince Angela that Oliver should live inside full-time, I would have been doing a disservice to every member of that multi-species family, especially Oliver.

Every animal, every situation, deserves a communicator who is willing to set their own opinions aside and hear exactly what the animal(s) have to say. Some of your deeply-held opinions may have to soften or dissolve for you to do this work.

There is no shortage of hot-button issues regarding the roles and relationships between animals and humans, and you'll eventually encounter them all. Be aware of your own hot buttons,

Lesson Eight: Common Blocks, Digging Deeper

and beware of statements (and even thoughts) that contain words like should, always, and never.

We can all agree that animal abuse and neglect are never (there's that word again) okay. But in order to do our best for each animal who entrusts us to understand and relay their truth, we have to be willing to set our opinions about everything else aside and meet each animal and human and situation exactly where they are.

🐾 Another block is circumstance.

Some times and places and situations just aren't conducive to clear communication. One of the most difficult situations—and yet most important for business-building—is doing animal communication at public events.

Quite often, I offer my services at public events. I've had booth space at community gatherings, agility trials, psychic fairs, and other public events. These events can be noisy, busy, and hectic. People will be waiting in line with their animals. People next to you or passing by will be loud and obnoxious. People will interrupt you.

Dogs will bark incessantly. Loudspeakers will boom with announcements. You'll have to be "on" all day. You'll have to have your shields up and your focus sharp to keep from being distracted. And of course, the animals you're working with will be distracted, too.

🐾 **Sometimes, you're just not all that high on a** dog's **list of fun things to do.**

Early in my career as a professional animal communicator, I was invited by a fellow communicator to participate in a Dog Fair in Houston, Texas. She had reserved the booth but then had a scheduling conflict. I was worried; I had never done back-to-back in-person readings at a public event before.

"Claim your power," she said, and so I did.

Things were going pretty well, until a young couple walked in with their young—and not-yet neutered—Doberman. The humans didn't have any real questions or concerns; they just wanted to confirm that their dog was happy with them and with his life. I couldn't get the dog's attention for love nor money. He was interested in everything outside the booth and nothing in it. His hormones were running high, his attention tuned to every female dog in the vicinity.

"Are you happy?" I asked him. "Yeah, yeah, yeah," he answered. "Do you like your people?" "Yeah, yeah, yeah," he answered. He wouldn't look at me or sit still for one second. I gave up. I didn't charge for the reading, and sent the people on their way with their distracted dog. When the couple and their dog were about 100 feet away, the dog looked over his shoulder at me. With his tail in the air, his butthole shining proudly in my direction, he said very clearly, "Well. That was stupid."

Lesson Eight: Common Blocks, Digging Deeper

When an animal isn't eager to communicate in a public setting, it's often hormonal—a female in heat, or a male with only one thing (or two or three things) on his mind.

Figure 32: *Our dog Bear was ruled by his hormones. Even after he was neutered, he managed to "hook up" with a female dog in estrus. I called the vet in a panic, but he assured me that Bear was shooting blanks.*

We used to joke about our dog Bear having a three-track mind: Can I eat it? Can I pee on it? Can I mount it? Even after he was neutered, he never lost that last compulsion. He was a very physical dog, not much interested in communicating anything beyond the fact that his food bowl was empty. He was a simple dog, and even though he wasn't a great communicator, it was easy to read his mind. If he ever made a beeline for a pretty girl sitting on the beach, I knew I had to run fast and get there before he could pee on her, thus marking her as his.

Especially when you're working with animals in-person at public events, you'll come across animals who just can't focus. Since my encounter with the distracted Doberman, I have learned a few tools to handle that issue.

I've learned not to set a time limit on public-event sessions, so the animal has the opportunity to settle down and relax before we get down to business. If, however, the animal is still antsy after about ten minutes, I will try to make an appointment for the animal's human to bring them back at another time, usually at the end of the event, so that by then most people have left and the environment isn't as stimulating. Or, I'll offer to do a remote session for their animal the next day, after I'm back at home.

When you're attempting to connect with an animal during a public event, or even at the animal's home, resist the urge to indulge in a lot of petting and physical contact. You don't need to touch an animal to connect with it. Physical contact can be a distraction (or outright dangerous).

Sitting quietly beside the animal, or across the room, works better than allowing it to climb all over you. It's helpful to remember that you're not trying to be a friend. You're not trying to be the human client's friend, either. You're just providing a

Lesson Eight: Common Blocks, Digging Deeper

line of communication between them. You don't need to win most-popular-among-animals-and-people awards.

Sometimes, eliminating distractions is all that's needed. When I'm working a public event, I have a 12 x 12 canopy outfitted with cloth sides that turn the canopy into an enclosed tent. This cuts down on visual distractions. Then, I allow the animal to explore the space until he's settled down and ready to communicate.

When someone brings more than one dog to my booth at the same time (or when I'm working with several animals in their home environment), one animal may insist on hogging my attention. If this happens, I ask the human-in-charge to bring the animals to me one at a time, so each one has their turn to communicate without having to fight for attention.

The trick is to be sensitive to the nuances of the animal's (and human's) behavior and determine what's getting between you, them, and the communication you're seeking. If you can get past your ego and your worry that you might be less-than-amazing, you'll be better able to figure out what's blocking communication.

You and your issues (multitudinous as they may be) aren't always the problem. Sometimes, the animal has to get past its own blocks to communication. When I can tell that the animal needs help getting into the right frame of mind before he can settle to communicate, I will often do a little energy healing first (after asking permission, of course). That usually does the trick.

Drawbacks and benefits of Remote vs In-Person Sessions

Remote sessions and in-person sessions both have benefits and drawbacks, and these relate to the block created by circumstance. Remote sessions can be easier than in-person sessions because you aren't contending with as many distractions.

However, sometimes in remote sessions, the animal can't tell you everything you need to know, and you'll have to connect in-person to get the full picture. I find that this happens most often when there is something in the environment that is contributing to the situation, but for whatever reason the animal isn't able to tell you what it is.

This can happen for several reasons. The animal may not know what the problem is. (Like the haunted labradoodle who didn't know what was happening to cause her fear.)

Other times, the animal knows that their human doesn't want them to spill the beans, so they dance around the question, hoping you can solve the equation without knowing the value of X.

In these situations, making a house call can give you a clue that will help you to ask the perfect question to unlock the flood gates. The animal's home environment can provide the bridge between the animal's inability to communicate the problem, and the communicator's inability to ask the right questions.

Lesson Eight: Common Blocks, Digging Deeper

If you don't live close enough to your client to make a house call, you may have to work with another animal communicator who lives closer. That's why it's good to belong to a network of communicator friends who are willing to help each other.

A lot of what I'm saying boils down to this: If you can't move the boulder, go around it. And if you can't find a way around it, figure out how to move it.

The Look of Communication

There's a particular look most animals get when they're communicating. They will settle in a relaxed position and their faces will have a quiet, soft-focused, inward-looking expression. Or, their eyes will close entirely, and they may even fall asleep. Many people report that it is obvious to them when their animal companions are communicating with me remotely. I always give the exact time of the communication in the transcript so they can validate their impression.

When you're communicating in-person, some animals will look at you directly. Others may noodle around the space and still answer your questions. But if you're trying to talk to a dog who's bouncing off the walls, forget it.

Animals who are receiving energy healing will often yawn, stretch, lick their lips, or if water is available, they'll get up to take a drink.

Hear Them Speak

In lesson two, there is a photo of a fox whose faraway expression shows that he is communicating. When you see that look, you'll know you're "in." Here are some other photos that show what animals look like when they are communicating.

Lesson Eight: Common Blocks, Digging Deeper

Figure 33: *Notice that Zuma isn't looking at me, though it is clear that he is connected-in telepathically. Animals who are communicating will often stare into space instead of looking at you. Photo by Therese Clinton.*

Figure 34: *Notice Zuma's faraway expression. Animals who are communicating often get a faraway look in their eyes and an expression of going-inward on their faces. Photo by Therese Clinton.*

Lesson Eight: Common Blocks, Digging Deeper

Figure 35: Tomo paced along the edges of his enclosure while communicating, but he still had that same faraway look on his face. Photo by Therese Clinton.

Figure 36: *Sometimes the animal will look directly at you while communicating, and it will be obvious from their expression that they are paying attention to you. Photo by Therese Clinton.*

Lesson Eight: Common Blocks, Digging Deeper

Figure 37: *Animals who are experiencing a shift during energy healing will often yawn. Photos by Therese Clinton.*

Blasting Through Blocks

Recognizing what is blocking you is the first step—and sometimes the only step necessary—to dismantling it.

If the block is your own emotional or physical state, take the time to get yourself healthy and clear. Meditate, get plenty of rest, exercise, and good nutrition. Do what it takes to protect yourself from disruptive influences in your life.

If the animal, or the animal's human, is blocking subconsciously, energy healing can help. If the human is blocking you, a frank but delicately-worded conversation might be necessary. Or, you may have to chalk that one up to something-beyond-my-control.

If your judgments or opinions are blocking you (or feeding you misinformation), that's on you. Learning animal communication will put you on a spiritual path that will help you to ditch some of your tendencies to judge others. But after all, you'll always be human, so it's always good to check in with yourself to make sure you're clear of agendas before beginning any communication session.

Circumstance is a big block that's fortunately easy to fix. Be aware of the pitfalls and benefits of both remote and in-person sessions, and take steps to create an environment that is as calm and distraction-free as possible. If a remote session isn't giving you all the clues you need to ask the right questions, offer to

Lesson Eight: Common Blocks, Digging Deeper

make a house call. If an in-person session has too many distractions, offer to do a remote session later.

In many cases, sending healing energy before the session can help to dismantle blocks, even those you can't quite identify. Getting energy healing for yourself can help, too.

Don't forget to do your centering/grounding/protecting ritual before every session. You may have to do it again in the middle of a session if you find that you are not connecting in as deeply as you would like.

LESSON EIGHT HIGHLIGHTS

🐾 In this lesson, we explored the most common blocks to effective communication. The first step—and sometimes the only step necessary—to blasting through blocks is to recognize them.

🐾 Strong emotion can block communication, whether it is coming from the animal, the animal's human, or the animal communicator. Worry over worst-case scenarios can cause a communicator to imagine the worst and then think it is coming from the animal.

🐾 Strong opinions on the part of the communicator can cause a communicator to project their agenda into the communication.

🐾 Circumstance can block communication, but once recognized can be easily fixed.

🐾 Animals who are communicating often get a certain faraway look that is easy to spot.

🐾 Higher-order needs, on the part of the animal or the communicator, can block communication.

Lesson Eight: Common Blocks, Digging Deeper

LESSON EIGHT TASKS

Well! Another big lesson done. Celebration is definitely in order! We dug deeper into the most common blocks to clear communication and learned how to blast through those blocks. Your daily practice sessions should start yielding even more clarity going forward.

1. Finally, it's time to go back and look at all the sessions you've done so far, and see if you can flip some of those red-marked passages to green.

2. Read those red-marked passages in your previous communications, and see if you can identify the blocks you may have been experiencing. The first step in fixing something is identifying the problem, so see if you can identify the block for every communication you felt you weren't getting quite right. Was the problem with you, the animal, the animal's human, or the situation? Or was it something else? Did you ask the wrong question?

3. Do a little writing about the communications you've had so far, and see if you can figure out what you were doing right when you felt "on" and what you could have done differently (if anything) when you felt "off."

4. Check back in with the animals in those not-quite-right communications, and try again. Write about that, too. Was it different? How was it different? What did you do differently this time?

5. If you haven't already been practicing in-person sessions, start now. This week, and for the rest of this course, do at least half of your animal communication sessions with a live animal in front of you. Your own animal companions will be happy to help. You can also communicate with the local wildlife. Go to a shelter or zoo or aquarium. Don't forget to chat with snakes, insects, spiders... in fact, just for grins, have a conversation in-person with a critter you're afraid of (just keep your distance!).

6. Write about hot-button issues regarding animals, and whether your opinions could stand in the way of receiving clear communication. We've already discussed a few potential subjects for you to explore further, but also consider these along with any others you think of: wild animals kept in captivity, trained/working animals, shelter adoption vs. buying from a breeder, raising farm animals to provide meat, land ownership and development vs. wildlife and ecology conservation, wild-horse roundups, biblical understanding of animals and the human/animal relationship, reincarnation, animals and the afterlife.

LESSON NINE: Troubleshooting

In lesson eight, we learned about the more common blocks to communication. In this lesson, we will dig deeper and explore some more specific blocks you may encounter, why they happen, and how to blast through them.

Figure 38: *Your own animal companions are happy to help you practice your animal communication skills and move past any blocks you have. But if you need more animal helpers, consider visiting your local animal shelter. You can do a lot of good there, even without bringing home new family members.*

Every Failure is an Opportunity

Knowing the common blocks to communication and taking steps to combat them, you will still experience failure. You will still experience moments of murkiness, when you're not sure you're getting correct information. Think of these moments as opportunities to develop your skills even further.

The cure for failure or doubt is to keep practicing.

Over time, you will fine-tune your ability to know when you are connected and when you're not. You'll feel the subtle shift that occurs when you begin to veer off track, so you can auto-correct.

In my years of teaching and mentoring others, I've noticed some specific problems that can occur on the journey to proficiency. If the blocks to communication we covered last week were boulders, these are rocks, maybe even pebbles. Still big enough to stub your toe or make you slip and fall. Fortunately, there are easy solutions.

The first step toward finding a solution is to recognize that something is blocking you from achieving clarity. The next step is to identify what's blocking you. Only then can you take steps to remove the obstacle.

This week, we'll dig in to more specific issues that may crop up to block your emerging skills. We'll discuss how each of these issues is experienced, what they mean, and how to deal with them.

Lesson Nine: Troubleshooting

We'll cover what to do when:

🐾 You've been having a slew of amazing, spot-on communication sessions and decided that you've *got* this, then you hit a spell of less-than-stunning results.

🐾 You've hit the wall and this whole endeavor seems like too much trouble or just not fun anymore.

🐾 You don't feel a telepathic connection to the animal.

🐾 You can communicate with everyone's animals but your own.

🐾 A visual image morphs from one thing to another, or appears fuzzy or unfocused.

🐾 You can't connect with the animals you meet out in the world.

🐾 You're experiencing success, and then your life falls apart.

When Amazing Success Slams into a Blank Wall of Nothing

You've been having a slew of amazing, spot-on communication sessions and decided that you've *got* this, then you hit a spell of less-than-stunning results. What went wrong, and what can you do about it?

This can happen for several reasons. The first three are sort of balled into one: Fear of success, fear of change, fear of what others may say.

Intuitive abilities like telepathy are intimately entwined with our sense of self, as are creative abilities like writing and art. When we begin to bring these long-hidden parts of ourselves into the light, we upset the status quo. All sorts of belief systems—ours and our loved-ones'—are challenged by the new person we are becoming. Our activities invite comment and criticism from others, and we may find ourselves under attack for our choices. Like a turtle who has stuck his head out only to find the world outside his shell is less hospitable than he'd hoped, we pull ourselves back into a space of safety.

When I teach a class, I hand out questionnaires at the end. To the question "What surprised you?" Most people answer "I was surprised I could do this." They paid money, set aside a weekend, showed up, and participated, but deep-down they didn't really think they would be able to communicate with animals.

Lesson Nine: Troubleshooting

If the hope you felt when you started this course was built on top of a subconscious fear of success, you might now be dealing with a whole slew of baggage you hadn't known existed.

It's easy to take a course, fail, and decide that the course was poorly designed or you're just not talented enough to make the grade. It is much harder to accept the fact that you have an ability that could change the world—or at least, your world—if you decide to do what it takes to embrace it.

What's the cure?

There are several. First, I always advise writing about anything that's hanging you up. A few pages of stream-of-consciousness inquiry can point you in the right direction to locate and unpack your baggage.

Second, don't take yourself so seriously. Practice an easy shrug and a quick answer you can employ when others (or even you) question your emerging abilities or your sanity.

Here are some common questions—and easy answers:

"Why are you doing this?" = "It interests me."

"You're wasting your time." = "I've wasted time before, and I'll probably waste time again. I doubt it'll kill me."

"Have you gone crazy?" = "Possibly."

"You can't really believe animal communication is real." = "I don't know yet. I'm finding out for myself. I'll let you know what I decide."

"Prove it." = "Send me a picture of your dog and a list of questions, and I'll try."

"So now you're going to be psychic and start reading my mind?" = "Oh, I've already done that. It wasn't very interesting, though, so I think I'll stick to communicating with animals from now on."

When the Path of Adventure Becomes a Pointless Uphill Trudge

I don't know why, but it seems to be human nature to want to abandon (or sabotage) anything that starts to smell like success. Your writing may have uncovered your particular reasons, and if so, unpack them, throw them on the trash heap, then buy a good lighter and set them on fire.

If you aren't sure what your reasons are, maybe it will help to explore mine:

Culprit: Lack of Emotional Energy

If you've hit the wall even though you and everyone else in your life are completely on-board with animal communication (and you're sure no monsters are lurking under the bed), you may have used up your energy reserves. Telepathy takes a lot of energy, even though you're mostly sitting in one place with your eyes closed.

Lesson Nine: Troubleshooting

Ask yourself: Have you been...?

...taking the time to refill your creative well?

...going outside, seeing and doing and trying new things?

...getting enough rest and relaxation?

...eating healthy food?

...taking care of business /clearing out your to-do list?

...managing your stress levels in a healthy way?

...meditating?

...protecting your time and energies?

...keeping good boundaries?

...being kind to yourself?

...valuing yourself by saying no when you need to?

Figure 39: *Good advice from Zen Kitty Princess Grace: Take the time to care for yourself, and rest when you need to. You can't be a clear channel if you're tired.*

Lesson Nine: Troubleshooting

Culprit: Perfectionism

You might hit the wall because you've experienced a measure of success, and now you expect yourself to be the best animal communicator in the universe. If you're a perfectionist, you have my deepest sympathies. I suffer from perfectionism, too, and I can tell you that as a writer, an artist, and even an animal communicator, perfectionism can be crippling. There ought to be a twelve-step group for perfectionists. (I wouldn't go—I'm not much of a joiner, but...)

Please give yourself the gift of being a beginner. If you've been judging yourself or your abilities—positive or negative; judgment is a block—or comparing yourself to other communicators, stop.

Give yourself time to find out who *you* are as a communicator. You are not (and won't ever be) exactly the same as anyone else. You will attract the animals you can help and the clients who will understand you. When you attract anything other than that, you're giving yourself a chance to stretch your skills and grow as a communicator. Comparing yourself to experts and deciding you could never measure up is like drinking poison.

Repeat after me: "I am opening up to a whole new world that I don't yet understand completely. I will allow myself to be a beginner for as long as it takes."

Trust yourself. You may be a beginner, but that doesn't mean you aren't good. Some of my most amazing animal communication stories are from my first year of practice, and my beginning students regularly experience incredible accuracy in class.

If you find yourself thinking or saying "I can't..." or "I'm not good at..." get a rubber band, put it on your wrist, and snap it forcefully against your skin whenever you dare to disrespect yourself that way. You don't know what you're good at until you have tried, allowed yourself to fail, and then tried again at least a thousand times.

Figure 40: *When Gabrielle met Opus during an animal communication class at Dragonfly Pond Farm, Opus communicated, "I want to go home with you!" Gabrielle was reluctant to tell me, but I already knew Opus wanted the opportunity to try out a new lifestyle with a trusted friend. It would have been a terrible shame if Gabrielle had blocked—or talked herself out of—the communication she received. You will be asked to broach potentially delicate subjects. Be mindful how you deliver sensitive information, but don't hold back when an animal asks you to tell their human companion something important.*

Lesson Nine: Troubleshooting

When You Don't Feel a Telepathic Connection

First, check your posture. Are you relaxed, feet on the floor, leaning back in a receptive way rather than forward in a projecting way? Is your mind clear? Did you take the time to get centered, grounded, and protected? Is anything churning in your mind? Are you worried you won't do well, afraid you'll be wrong? Are you comparing yourself to someone else, trying to measure up to the best communicator on the planet instead of allowing yourself to be the best communicator you can be at this moment?

If you've checked your own mindset and determined that you are open and ready to receive but you're still not feeling connected, please resist the urge to feel that you're doing something wrong (or worse, that you're no good at this).

Sometimes, you won't feel a strong connection, even though you may be getting good, valid information. If you'll take it on faith and keep trying, you may ease into a better-feeling connection as the session rolls along. As with energy healing, don't get stuck on how it appears or on how it feels. Sometimes the connection will feel amazing. Other times, it'll seem more flat. But you may still be connected-in enough to get your questions answered.

Think of when you're talking to a stranger at a party. You may feel deeply connected to this person, or you may feel the connection is more superficial. But you can still hear what they're saying.

Like people, some animals are harder to connect with than others. It could simply be that you're trying to connect with an animal who isn't interested in talking with you. Try again tomorrow. Maybe tomorrow they—or you—will feel differently.

When Your Own Animal Companions Clam Up

Are you having trouble connecting with your own animals, or animals you know well, but seem to have an easier time with animals you've just met?

🐾 **It can be hardest to connect with the animals you know and love.**

Remember that one of the blocks to communication is strong emotion, and one of the strongest emotions is love. Even experienced communicators can have difficulty connecting with their own animals, especially when asking hard questions, such as whether the animal is ready to transcend this life.

Lesson Nine: Troubleshooting

Figure 41: *It can be hard to communicate with our own animals, especially when we worry they might tell us something we don't want to hear. When Jack started feeling bad, it was easy to tell through simple observation. What he wanted us to do for him (and when) was harder to hear, because my emotions were involved.*

- **When we are afraid of hearing the truth, it can block our reception.**

I had a hard time hearing my dog Jack when we were struggling to make end-of-life decisions for him. As I've advised you to do, when I didn't trust myself, I asked for help. My experienced animal communicator friends all told me he was ready to go.

I knew it myself, sometimes.

But I wasn't ready to let him go. I knew I never would be. I had the power to release him from his pain, but I couldn't convince myself that he was really, truly ready to be helped over the Rainbow Bridge. Though his body was failing him and he was in a lot of pain, his mind and emotions were still clear. There were so many things he could still do, and he could do them better than anyone. Benevolent Leader of all the animals at Dragonfly Pond Farm, and Best Good Dog Ever, Jack was the glue that kept our multispecies tribe operating smoothly. He'd been training Jed to take his place for over a year, but we all, especially Jed, knew that Jed wasn't yet ready to assume the reins of power.

But Jack's body was betraying us all. He couldn't navigate the stairs, and even on level ground, his back leg would collapse under him unexpectedly, cruelly twisting his spine.

Was Jack ready to go? His body said yes. His mind, and his enormous heart, said no.

Jack was as conflicted as I was over the decision. He was also afraid of what would happen during the drug-induced transition we were considering. Would it hurt? Would we all regret the decision the moment the heart-stopping drug entered his system?

I didn't know those answers. I only knew that the pain he was experiencing every day was almost more than *I* could stand. Which meant I wasn't emotionally detached enough to be sure I was making the right decision. I needed Jack to make the final decision.

I explained the physical process of euthanasia to Jack. I promised that I'd hold his paw and stay connected to his spirit even after his heart stopped beating. I showed him the crowd of beloved animal and human companions who waited for him to run across the Rainbow Bridge. I knew we'd all celebrate the moment when all four of his paws were able to dig deep and leap high, free of pain and limitation.

But there was no escaping the fact that he'd have to walk over the bridge into the hereafter by himself. That scared him. It scared me, too.

It made letting go that much harder for both of us.

All the available evidence told me that Jack was past ready to go. Even if he hadn't told me of his suffering, I would have been able to see it. But because I loved him too much to really let go, there was no way I could ever be clear enough to know for sure that any decision I made would be the right one. Even now, with my own superpowers of animal communication and the support and advice of some talented animal communicators with whom I would trust MY life; a tiny, doubting part of me will always wonder whether I made that decision too early, or too late.

A big part of being a good animal communicator lies in understanding your limitations. Sometimes, you won't know the right answer. Because sometimes, there isn't one.

Figure 42: *Jack looking through the window when he was in too much pain to play outside.*

Your animal companion may be reluctant to say something you don't want to hear. They may be determined to hold on until letting go becomes not only possible, but imperative. Or, you may be blocking yourself because of a strong desire to help your beloved animal, or an animal you've come to love.

When you feel a strong emotional connection to any animal or human, you may be concerned that you'll hear something you'd rather not hear, or have to tell something you'd rather not tell. I'm sorry to say that in many cases, there is no easy answer. Try to release your agendas and open your heart to whatever comes, then surrender the need to control what happens. It won't be easy. The only promise I have to offer is that while it won't be easy, it might be possible. Just let go and do your best. That's all any of us can do.

When an Image Morphs from One Thing to Another

Sometimes, we receive an image, then the image morphs, or flickers, into a different image. These images can be similar, such as a toy mouse vs. a real mouse, or completely different, such as a mountaintop vs. the ocean.

This "morphing-image" problem can happen when the rational/thinking/projecting part of your brain argues with the feeling/knowing/intuition part of your brain.

Whether or not these processes occur exclusively in the left-brain or right-brain may be under debate among experts, but which part of the brain does the work doesn't matter. What does matter is that there are two distinct ways of processing information. In this book, for the purpose of explanation, I'll stick to the left-brain vs. right-brain theory as a consciousness concept, and leave the neuroscience to the experts.

The left-brain consciousness works in a linear, methodical way. It is concerned with past and future, with separating and categorizing and projecting past events into potential future possibilities. It is the "I am" consciousness that differentiates each of us as an individual being and separates us from everyone else.

The right-brain consciousness works in a freewheeling, global way. It is concerned with the present moment, with connecting us to the collective consciousness that unites us all. It is "the witness" consciousness that sees itself as a small, indivisible fragment of all-that-is.

When we receive telepathic information, we're opening our consciousness to a right-brain collage of sensory information. Then, the left brain categorizes and makes sense of the information. Usually, when we "get it wrong" it is because the right brain has received the correct information, but the left brain has interpreted it incorrectly. Or, the left brain leaps to answer the question before the right brain has the chance to connect-in.

The morphing-image problem can occur when both sides of the brain are trying to answer the same question using different information. The right brain may be connecting with the animal and seeing the collage of information while the left brain is figuring out a likely answer based on available information, past experience, and potential outcomes.

Can the right brain information we receive be wrong? Yes, if we're not connected to the animal and are instead receiving information from another animal or human who is nearby or emotionally involved. It is also possible that we're receiving some

Lesson Nine: Troubleshooting

information from the animal, and some information from the animal's human, so we are receiving two different images at the same time, and therefore the image in our mind's eye seems to flicker between one thing and another.

This is especially likely when we're dealing with a lost animal. The animal may be showing us where they are (or where they've been), while the animal's emotionally involved human is inadvertently showing us their worst possible fears, or highest hopes for a good outcome.

The morphing-image problem can also happen when there is more than one "answer" to the question, or when the animal doesn't know the answer, or even when the animal is playing or pretending something.

I once spoke with a cat who showed me an image of himself playing with a mouse. The image kept morphing between a real mouse and a toy mouse. Rather than agonize over which was correct, I talked to the cat's human, who provided two pieces of information: One, the cat lived inside 24/7. Two, the cat loved to pounce-on and "kill" his toy mouse and carry it around the house like a trophy which he would then lay in front of his mistress as a gift. Exactly the same thing an outdoor cat would do with a real mouse.

To solve the mystery of a morphing image, ask the animal, or the animal's human, if they know which of the images you're seeing is correct. Most of the time, one of them will be able to tell you.

When an Image Appears Fuzzy or Unfocused

If you're getting a fuzzy image, it can be because the animal is showing you a snapshot of something that it didn't see clearly.

Once, I was communicating with a little dog who showed an image of himself being whacked on the butt with a rolled-up magazine. The dog's human, a woman, wanted to know which of her boyfriends (current or past) had done the deed. The dog didn't show me the person's face—it was a big, squareish, hairy blur. Beard, maybe, I couldn't tell for sure. All I could see clearly from the dog's vantage point on the floor looking straight up was a big hand holding the magazine, and a big belly encased in a flannel shirt with straining buttons. That was enough of a description for the woman to know which boyfriend it was. Luckily, it was the one she had already kicked to the curb.

You might also get a blurry image when you're trying too hard. First, do a quick self-check to see if you're the problem.

🐾 How to Know You're Open & Receptive

> You're sitting in an open, receptive position, leaning back, feet on floor, hands, face and body relaxed. Your mind is calm; you are feeling emotionally neutral.

Lesson Nine: Troubleshooting

🐾 How to Know You're Trying Too Hard

You're leaning forward, curled inward, legs and/or arms crossed, fingers clenched, face scrunched in thought, body tense. Your mind is churning, reaching for information, or trying to "figure it out." You are anxious, worried, or feeling an excess of any other emotion.

Determine that the problem isn't you, and if it is, fix the problem.

Then, ask the animal to tell you in words what they just showed you. Or, ask them to show the picture again more clearly. Ask open-ended questions to find out why the animal is sending (or you're seeing) a fuzzy or blurry picture.

There is a third possibility—you're making stuff up. This does happen, especially when you're first starting out, and you haven't yet figured out how your imagination feels different from true communication. Time and practice will help.

But even seasoned professionals have to watch for this pitfall. Sometimes we are working events that last all day—or several all-days in a row. I've been to events when I was so busy I didn't have time to eat. (I've learned to bring snacks.) It's easy to get tired and stop connecting-in as deeply.

Hear Them Speak

You May Not Always Be Up for Communication.

You might receive unfocused images because you aren't clear yourself. You may be too tired, coming down with a cold, or distracted by something else going on in your life. If you've determined that this isn't the problem, and you're concerned that you may be making things up, check your posture. Check your emotions. And if you're still not feeling "on," remember, it is fine (in fact, it's preferred) if you say, "I don't know. It's blurry, it's fuzzy. I'm not sure what I'm getting." You're not Spider Man or Harry Potter. You WILL sometimes be wrong. Get over it.

When You Can't Connect with Animals You Happen to Meet

Figure 43: This belligerent rooster may not want to communicate with you. That's okay. Every animal you see doesn't have to be your new best friend because you're an animal communicator.

Lesson Nine: Troubleshooting

When I first started taking my abilities seriously and working to improve them, I wondered why I couldn't connect with every animal I saw out in the world. When I took my first big several-days-long workshop, I sort of expected that when we had a day off and I went into town, I'd suddenly be communicating with every dog I walked past, every squirrel or bird that crossed my path. It didn't happen.

Over time, I realized that my expectation had been unrealistic.

Compare animal communication to human communication. When a toddler is just learning to speak, they will chatter to anyone, even complete strangers. But then they become socialized to the fact that it isn't appropriate to speak to everyone they see.

In public, a friendly smile is about the most communication that passes between strangers. Only very occasionally will people who don't know each other strike up a conversation. I've made friends by talking to the person standing next to me in the grocery store line. But that sort of thing is rare, even for a gregarious introvert like me. Most of the time, I go about my business and expect others to go about theirs.

It's the same with animals. Not all of them are interested in striking up a conversation with a stranger. Some will be; some are very surprised when a human connects with them, and they're excited and want to explore the novelty of human telepathic communication. It's as fun for them as it is for you! Some can tell you're able to communicate, and they'll connect with you before you even notice them. I've had squirrels and birds, even dragonflies, come up to me with something to say. Dogs, too, though usually their humans are busy dragging them away and apologizing for the dog's forward manner.

Some animals would be willing, but they don't expect it, so they don't recognize that you're attempting to connect. They greet you the way they greet everyone else; the animal equivalent of a nod and a smile.

Penelope Smith said, "Only go where you're invited." Meaning, it really isn't appropriate for us to reach out to every animal we see. Dogs walking on leash with their humans are really sort of off-limits unless you tell the dog's human companion that you are a communicator and ask if they'd like you to connect with the dog. Or unless the dog just offers up some information they want you to share with their person.

Another thing that happens is, unless animals have something important to say, they often won't say anything. They don't go around chattering about their thoughts the way humans do. Their minds are quieter, less cluttered. Sometimes they're just experiencing being in their bodies and observing the world. Some animals won't share anything unless you ask a specific question about something that matters to them. If they don't know you, and you're not the chosen conduit between them and their human, they don't see the point in sharing their innermost feelings.

So, if you can't spontaneously read every passing thought of every passing animal, it doesn't mean you're doing anything wrong. That's just not the way telepathic communication works.

When You're Making Significant Progress (and Suddenly Your Life Falls Apart)

Learning to communicate telepathically with animals is a spiritual path. And if you've also been meditating, and/or doing yoga, and/or getting energy work, you're moving a ton of energy through your body-mind-spirit. You are clearing the decks so you can become an even better and more effective channel of communication.

Old baggage that you haven't quite let go of is bound to come up for review. Chaos often precedes transformation. It's a push-pull of two different aspects of the self, at war over who you will become.

There is a small, frightened part of you that thinks anything new and different is so scary that it must stop your evolution from continuing, because the status quo feels safe. Ever since our days as cave-dwellers, we have been hardwired to avoid the dangerous unknown.

There is an expanded, all-knowing part of you that is presenting you with the past baggage that has weighed you down and given you a contracted, stunted view of who you are and what you can achieve. It wants you to face and dismantle your illusions of limitation and the wrong-headed assumptions you have absorbed from others. These seemingly-opposite aspects of self are throwing roadblocks in your way. One wants you to run and hide. The other knows you can face and conquer anything.

Old, toxic relationships and patterns may reemerge while you are immersed in the deep spiritual process of recovering your ability to communicate with animals. If you are experiencing chaos in your life as a result of your spiritual path, I encourage you to find a trusted mentor, spiritual advisor, healer, or therapist to shepherd you through this challenging but rewarding time in your life.

Lesson Nine: Troubleshooting

LESSON NINE HIGHLIGHTS

🐾 When you've been having a slew of amazing, spot-on communication sessions, then hit a spell of less-than-stunning results, it can be because of a fear of success, fear of change, or fear of what others may say. When this happens, write about it, and try not to take yourself too seriously.

🐾 When it feels like you've hit the wall, you could be suffering from perfectionism, or a lack of emotional energy. When this happens, try to take better care of yourself, avoid comparing yourself to others, and give yourself permission to be a beginner.

🐾 When you don't feel a telepathic connection to the animal, you could still be getting good information. Every communication won't have the same degree of clarity. Sometimes, you may have to take it on faith and verify with the animal's human later.

🐾 When it seems that you can communicate with everyone's animals but your own, you may be blocking because you are worried about what you might learn. And, if your animals are worried about how you'll take what they have to say, they may clam up.

- 🐾 When a visual image morphs from one thing to another, the rational/thinking/projecting part of your brain may be arguing with the feeling/knowing/intuition part of your brain. It can also happen when there is more than one "answer" to the question, or when the animal doesn't know the answer, or even when the animal is playing or pretending something.

- 🐾 When an image appears fuzzy or unfocused, the animal could be showing something that it didn't see clearly. Or, you could be trying too hard, or not in the right frame of mind to communicate.

- 🐾 When you are out in the world and can't connect with the animals you meet, it's because that just isn't the way it works.

- 🐾 When you're experiencing success, then your life falls apart, old baggage is coming up for review. Unpack it, bless it, release it, and you will achieve more clarity in all of your sessions going forward.

Lesson Nine: Troubleshooting

LESSON NINE TASKS

This week, we explored some specific issues involving the ability to receive clear information. The tasks this week are designed to help you process and clear any of these issues, as well as any others that may have cropped up for you.

1. Write about any blocks you've encountered that haven't been covered in the book. Use your intuition to come up with an explanation or solution.

2. Has any old baggage resurfaced? Could it be related to your fears about becoming an animal communicator? Could it be a chance to bless and release something from your past that you've been holding onto?

3. Sometime this week, make the time to do a few fun things you haven't done in a while. Paint something! Plant something! Spend a day, or just an hour, just having fun.

4. Are you getting enough rest and relaxation? Be kind to yourself. Go to bed early! Sleep late! Take a nap! Get a massage!

5. Are you eating healthy and moderating your consumption of mood-altering substances? Are you using tobacco, drugs,

alcohol, sugar, or caffeine to manage your mood? If you know you need to moderate some of your less-than self-nurturing behaviors, please get help for anything truly serious. For the less-serious but still self-destructive behaviors, try substituting something else for any behavior that is getting out of hand. Have Kombucha instead of alcohol, herbal tea instead of coffee, a home-cooked gourmet meal instead of Twinkies and ice cream.

6. Have you been taking care of business so you don't have a huge to-do list on your mind? Knock out your to-do list, and then do something extra. Cleaning out a closet can go a long way toward uncluttering your mind.

7. Are you meditating? Meditation has so many health benefits, but it's the first thing to go by the wayside when our lives get too hectic. Yet ironically, that's when we need it most.

8. Are you protecting your time and energies? Keeping good boundaries? Value yourself and your abilities by saying no when you need to. Notice whether you're self-sabotaging by taking on more things than you have time to say grace over.

LESSON TEN: Communicating with Clients and Counseling Multispecies Families

This week, we will cover some practical and ethical considerations you'll encounter as a counselor in multi-species relationships.

Figure 44: *How many dogs in this picture? (Hint: It's not two.) Just another blended family with more animals than people. What could possibly go wrong?*

Hear Them Speak

Knowing What to Say

Before you open your mouth to speak with a client, ask yourself these questions: Is it true? Is it kind? Is it necessary? Even if the information you have to relay passes these tests, you may have to tread carefully on wording and delivery. An alienated client is of no benefit to the animal you're trying to help. And yet, you must relay the truth of what you see. Telling a person what they want to hear and agreeing with them even when they're wrong doesn't help anyone.

Figure 45: *This stray puppy is being trained by our cat Max. He learned to love cats but was a determined chicken-killer; his way of showing us that he would make a better city dog. Every home an animal lands in isn't supposed to be theirs forever. You may have to counsel families on finding the right fit for an animal who wants to live somewhere other than where they are.*

Lesson Ten: Communicating with Clients and Counseling Multispecies Families

🐾 An animal communicator is part translator, part therapist, part lawyer, part investigator, part social worker, part healer.

You will have to translate between animals and humans, then back again between humans and animals. You will have to give wise counsel to both sides, mediate differences, and draw up agreements between all parties. The telepathic part of the job is only the beginning, but it is the essential bit that makes all the others possible. One of the biggest challenges in being an animal communicator is—you guessed it—communicating with humans.

It is no surprise that dogs, cats, horses and all manner of animals are fed-up with people. Quite often, I'm not overly fond of us, either. People can be incredibly dense, so self-involved that they can't see past the pimple on the end of their nose. Communicating with clients who don't want to see what's going on is a special challenge.

Sometimes, humans don't want the truth. They only want support for their own viewpoint. Or, they want the truth if it's convenient and doesn't cost too much in time, money, or effort. Sometimes, they want permission, or to feel better about something they've done or decided to do.

But most of the time, people who come to you want and deserve your help. They may have felt compelled to seek animal communication even though they, personally, don't believe. It can be because they have tried everything else and nothing worked. It can be because their animal led them to you.

To rise above the seeming contradictions of human behavior, it helps to avoid judgment.

Understanding People

You will come across people who want to test you, even set you up for failure, so they can convince themselves that animal communication is (or isn't) real. Usually when that happens, it isn't because the person is mean and sneaky. Often, it is because they want to convince themselves before trusting you with their deepest-darkest secrets and fears.

🐾 Judge not, judge not, judge not.

A crusty old man at a psychic fair showed me a picture of his dog and asked me to tell him how she was doing, health-wise. I connected-in and told him about her hip dysplasia and heart murmur.

The man (let's call him The Jerk) shouted, "Ha!" so loud that people stopped what they were doing and looked over at my table. He chortled that he'd proven me to be a fake because the dog had been dead for two years.

I explained that animal communication isn't bound by space or time, or even life or death, and that I could easily speak with his

Lesson Ten: Communicating with Clients and Counseling Multispecies Families

dog whether she was still in physical form or not. I asked if the answers I had given him were accurate of the dog's health issues when she was alive.

The man's smug smile faltered. He even teared up a little. I asked if he would like to start over and ask some questions he really wanted to know the answers to. His wall of arrogance tumbled down, and he nodded.

We started the session again, and the man said that he had accidentally run over his dog. The image he described of her death throes was vivid and upsetting. I explained how, in moments of extreme and unexpected trauma, an animal's spirit will fly away from the body. I explained that what he had witnessed was just the body's physical processes shutting down. I assured him that his dog hadn't suffered. I gave a detailed visual of her spirit leaping and playing in the yard outside his mobile home, and the man's last shred of resistance melted away.

The dog let me know that she had prompted the man to come and speak with me so I could help him heal and move on with his life. At the end of the session, he walked out of the room without talking with any of the other psychics.

He had only come there to see me.

Now, don't you feel bad that we called him a jerk? Because he was just a poor old man who missed his dog, and needed me to prove that I could, in fact, connect with his beloved companion before he could release his guilt and grief.

🐾 Most of the time, you will succeed. Sometimes, you will fail.

When you do fail even after you've tried everything, be willing to admit defeat and refer your client to someone else. Knowing when you can't help *is* a help.

In all the years I've been doing this, I've only experienced a handful of times when a combination of animal communication and healing failed to solve a problem. But failure is a fact of life. Marriage counselors fail to save marriages. Doctors and psychiatrists fail to save clients from disease or self-destruction. Social workers fail to save the children or elderly or disadvantaged people in their caseload. Energy healers fail, and so do animal communicators. I have failed, and you will, too.

I failed when a guy who enlisted my help wasn't interested in hearing what his animal companion had to say. When it turned out that his poor training practices were the cause of his dog's aggression, he didn't want to hear it. He didn't want help, if help involved him changing his ways. I don't know what happened to the dog. I won't ever know. I have to let that go.

Another time I failed was when the situation was a combination of environmental and behavioral patterns that neither I, nor the dog's very caring human companion, had much control over. My client's full-time job meant that she had to rely on other family members who weren't always willing to follow-through with suggestions for improvement. (You can't fault a dog for peeing in the house if no one will let him outside.)

Lesson Ten: Communicating with Clients and Counseling Multispecies Families

I failed to help a cat whose pee-spraying ways got him tossed outside for good. It took communication with all the other cats in the house (there were several) to find out who was doing the spraying, and all paws pointed to one cat. He couldn't tell me why he was spraying, except to say that he felt nervous all the time, and marking the house with his pee-spray made him feel better. But the other cats revealed the family's problems, one puzzle-piece at a time. Tempers were short among both humans and cats, and the home environment was chaotic. My offer of energy healing was refused; money was tight and it was easier to just toss out the offender.

> When one animal in a multi-species family begins acting-out, that animal may be the symptom-bearer of a larger problem that involves the whole family.

The animal who is seemingly at the center of the issue may have no idea what's causing him or her to act out, and the human can't see the plank in their own eye, while others in the family organism can be more objective.

I say family organism, because that's what a family is. An organism. Just as a collection of atoms make up molecules that make up cells that make up the body, each human and animal in a multi-species family has a part to play in whatever goes on. One person may seem to be unaffected, but that doesn't mean they're not involved.

In a family organism, an imbalance that affects the whole family may be shown through the disruptive behavior of one individual. Human or animal, this family member is the symptom bearer. Whether it's a child who's getting into trouble in school, a dog who's digging holes in the yard, or a cat who's peeing in the laundry basket, the symptom-bearer is no more guilty than every other family member. In fact, the symptom bearer is often the most tender-hearted and sensitive of the lot. They are, usually, just the first to break under the strain.

You can work with only the symptom bearer, but you're not likely to create full and permanent success this way. Things may get better for a while; in fact, they probably will, but the cure won't hold up long-term. Because the whole family is the problem, the whole family must be the solution. Unfortunately for the pee-spraying cat, his family wasn't willing to fix the core issues when it was easier to exile the symptom-bearer.

Communicators and healers can usually (not always) find the source of a problem, and we can usually (not always) direct energy healing that will help to dismantle unhealthy patterns. But sometimes, there are physical or behavioral components that we should refer out to other professionals. And even then, it takes a committed family to carry out a successful behavior-modification program.

Lesson Ten: Communicating with Clients and Counseling Multispecies Families

Wheeling and Dealing

A big part of the professional animal communicator's job is counseling multi-species families and coming up with agreed-upon solutions that will work for everyone. When someone fails to hold up their end of the deal, that someone is usually (always) the human.

I have to admit, I have done it myself. When my Scarlet Macaw, Talume, started projectile pooping outside his cage, I asked him nicely to stop. He declined. I asked why he was hell-bent on squirting streams of poop onto my clean-mopped tile floor.

His answer: "Why would I poop inside my cage? That's nasty!"

I had to concede Talume's point. I promised to clean his cage more often, but that wasn't a sweet-enough deal for him. He also wanted to be allowed more play time outside his cage. The deal we struck was that in return for not pooping inappropriately, he would get one hour of playtime outside his cage every day.

Parrots can be like toddlers; they will get into mischief if they're allowed outside their cages unsupervised. But I figured I could find the time to let him out while I cleaned the kitchen or folded laundry, so one hour of supervised playtime didn't seem like such a hardship.

Our agreement stuck for about a month. He got his hour of play time and stopped projectile pooping. Then, I got busy and started backsliding on my end of the deal. He put up with that for about a week. Then he went back to projectile pooping across the room.

Even animal communicators can get busy and stop listening to their animal family members. And when no one's listening, animals have two very powerful tools at their disposal to get your attention. Pee, and poop.

The underlying meaning in the way the message is conveyed is often pointedly direct. Inappropriate peeing is a very effective way to express the consciousness of being pissed-off.

An animal peeing on your bed—or God forbid, your pillow—is even madder than the one who pees on your shoes. They've been trying to get your attention for a long time, and you haven't been listening. They're saying, "Maybe *this* will get your attention."

While the method of attention-getting is common, the reasons for such behavior are many and varied, anything from physical ailments like bladder infections to manipulative attempts to coerce humans to do better. Finding out what the animal is trying to relay through their misbehavior is, of course, where animal communication comes in.

Communicating with Clients on Physical and Medical Matters

Animal communicators are not veterinarians—unless, of course, they are. And it is against the law for anyone without a veterinary license to practice veterinary medicine or to dispense veterinary advice. *So don't do it!*

Lesson Ten: Communicating with Clients and Counseling Multispecies Families

People will ask you to diagnose their animal. They will ask what they should do about this or that medical problem, which supplements they should give, and whether the animal has a problem that requires veterinary care. Your answer should always be: "If you think your animal has a medical problem, or you need advice about medications or dietary requirements, take your animal to the vet."

If you want to get really technical, you shouldn't even be advising that an animal needs to drink more water. In fact, unless you're a trained expert in the administration of supplements, oils, essences, or whatever, you are treading on thin ice if you are advising your clients to use those things. It's called *dispensing veterinary advice without a license.*

You *can* tell your client how their animal is feeling, and advise them to consult a veterinarian. You can say, "The dog hates the taste of his medicine; ask your vet if there's a better way to dose him." You can't say, "Stop giving him that medicine because he hates it."

I invite my clients to take the transcripts from my communication sessions to their veterinarian. Many do, and most vets welcome the added depth of knowledge, especially when they're dealing with vague symptoms. The information is provided for what it's worth, but I would never try to tell a veterinarian how to do his job. (They're not doing my job, why would I try to do theirs?)

> Animal communication, energy healing, and excellent veterinary care should work together. One doesn't replace another.

You will be asked to help with medical issues, and you can do that, as long as you remember your limits and boundaries, and don't overstep them. There are many ways that you can help with medical problems as an animal communicator.

When you're working with an animal who reveals a medical problem, if you're able to send healing energy, and you have the animal's permission, that's fine. But also advise your client, armed with the information you've given, to take their animal to the vet. Don't ever say, "I've healed your dog."

Pride and arrogance go before a fall, and if you're determined to fall, don't take the animal you're trying to help along with you. I give a healing session along with every communication, but I get the human's permission up-front before I even begin the session, and then I get the animal's permission before I proceed.

"But," you may ask, *"Doesn't everyone want to be healed? Why would anyone refuse healing?"*

Many people and animals don't want you to send healing energy to them. For people, there are often religious concerns. They feel that God is the only source of healing they can accept. If I were inclined to argue with that viewpoint, I could say that God is the source of all healing, even when it's being channeled

Lesson Ten: Communicating with Clients and Counseling Multispecies Families

through me. But by this point in my life, I'm not inclined to argue with anyone's religious views.

Others don't believe in energy healing or animal communication. And they won't be contacting you, so you won't need to worry about their views. But their spouse or someone close to them may ask for your help. *Never send healing energy to anyone, animal or human, without their knowledge and permission.* Now, if the relationship with a person or animal is part of another person's or animal's healing, that's different. You're not sending anything TO them.

Here's what I mean: If a woman asks you to help her and her dog heal from trauma they both experienced at the hands of her estranged husband, you can do that. The emotional scars from their relationship with the woman's husband will be addressed. The behavioral residue (the dog's aggression toward men, the woman's inability to trust) will be excised. However, if the woman asks you to send healing to the estranged husband so he will be a better person, that's not okay. That would mean you're trying to change a person who may not want to be changed.

Here's a personal story to even further illustrate the point. When one of my adult daughters was making life decisions that terrified me so much that it kept me up at night and made me less effective during the day, I tried to do energy healing for her, with the agenda of keeping her safe. (See my trying to control the universe and everyone in it?)

But in the energy healing protocol I use, the first question I muscle-test for is: "Do I have permission to do this?" In the case of me trying to interfere in my daughter's free will to make her own mistakes, the answer was always "No." A parent can consent to energy healing for their child, but not for an adult, even one they gave birth to.

Sometimes, the path to highest-and-best-good for a person or animal involves a period of suffering and slogging through the swamps of despair. Fault and failure—and even life-threatening illness—may be their chosen path. We sign on to the contract of life on earth to experience many things, and not all of them are pleasant.

Working with Animals Who Are Old or Ill

When animals have chronic health conditions that require medical care (old-age often being one of these) there are many decisions to be made. Often the decisions must be made over and over again as the situation evolves. These can be difficult decisions for an animal's human companion, and knowing the animal's wishes along the way can provide a great deal of comfort.

These communications go beyond conversations about minor aches, pains, and injuries, into more serious territory. How much is the animal willing to suffer in search of a cure? How will the dog who has just been hit by a car feel if he wakes from surgery

Lesson Ten: Communicating with Clients and Counseling Multispecies Families

to find that his leg has been amputated? Does the cat with cancer want to go through surgery and chemotherapy? Will the elderly animal who has stopped eating agree to be tube-fed? Will the animal with severe dehydration welcome weekly injections of subcutaneous fluids?

One of the great rewards of being an animal communicator is the opportunity to be an advocate for animals, as well as a support system for their human companions. This comes into sharp focus when end-of-life decisions are being made. It's gratifying to save an animal from early and unnecessary euthanasia, or to help an animal who is tired of suffering transition with ease and grace.

One of the difficulties with communicating in these situations is that the animal may be experiencing strong emotions (remember, strong emotions can block communication). The animal may be in pain or in shock. Either can make him so focused inward that he can't connect, or conversely, his spirit may have left the building even though his body is still functioning.

In these circumstances, you may be able to connect with the animal's higher self rather than their earthly consciousness. If you aren't able to connect with an animal who is suffering physically, ask if he will allow you to connect on a higher or more spiritual level. You'll either be given permission to connect or you won't. All you can do is try.

Helping to Make End-of-Life Decisions

Animal communicators are often called on to help people make end-of-life decisions for their animal companions. Obviously, these decisions are not to be made lightly. The yardstick questions "*Is it true? Is it kind? Is it necessary?*" become even more important. Your opinion doesn't matter. The opinion of the animal's human companion doesn't matter, either. The only opinion you need to hear and relay is the opinion of the animal you are communicating with.

When you are asked to help with end-of-life decisions, the only opinion that matters is that of the animal whose fate is being decided. And yet, it is also important not to judge the human who can't bring themselves to consider euthanasia, or the human who can't bear the burden of seeing their animal companion suffer for another minute.

Lesson Ten: Communicating with Clients and Counseling Multispecies Families

Figure 46: *Our dog Molly was ready to cross the Rainbow Bridge long before I was ready to let her go. Even though she told me her wishes many times, she still had "good days" that made me hesitate. I had to wait until I was absolutely sure that neither of us would change our mind at the last minute.*

Animal communication can help us to understand an animal's wishes, but the human-in-charge has to make the final decision, and it is never easy.

Some people will want your validation (and absolution) for decisions they've already made. Some will want to prolong their animal's life through heroic efforts. Some will want to provide euthanasia before the animal's illness complicates their lives. Some are too tender-hearted to see their companion suffer; others are too afraid of being left alone to let their loved one go.

In making life-and-death decisions, it is especially important to make sure that you are clear of agendas. If your agenda is to help the human feel better about their choices, you should recuse yourself from the case and ask another communicator to help. A multitude of emotional baggage may be involved in making this decision, including your own. But in the end, what the animal wants is the only thing that matters.

If the decision has been made to euthanize an animal, you as a communicator are uniquely suited to provide support, ease the transition for the grieving human, and assist the animal who is about to cross over.

Energy healing can help everyone (animal and human) release their blocks to making this momentous step. Promises and pacts can be dissolved so the animal won't feel obliged to hang on even though it is suffering. Emotional baggage can be unpacked and released for those leaving and those staying behind.

Lesson Ten: Communicating with Clients and Counseling Multispecies Families

Encountering Resistance

Eventually, you will run across someone who won't accept anything you tell them. They'll argue, or become defensive, or offer alternative interpretations for the information. This can happen when the person doesn't want to admit that they have a contributing role in the animal's behavior. Or, they don't want to accept the fact that their animal wants or needs something they are unwilling to give.

In these situations, it's best not to argue. But neither should you agree with a client just to be agreeable. All you can do is relay the information you've received, then let them do with it what they will.

Confidentiality

One final point about communicating with your clients is the importance of confidentiality. It is not okay to go around talking specifics about your clients or their animals or their situations. You can tell the cool animal-communication stories you'll accumulate, because you will have a lot of amazing tales to tell if you keep doing this! But without permission, you can't divulge the names of anyone or their animals. You cannot tell a story in a way that would identify a client if you were speaking to someone they know.

LESSON TEN HIGHLIGHTS

🐾 An animal communicator is part translator, part therapist, part lawyer, part investigator, part social worker, part healer.

🐾 Before you open your mouth to speak with a client, ask yourself these questions: Is it true? Is it kind? Is it necessary?

🐾 People can be difficult and complicated. Judge not, judge not, judge not.

🐾 Most of the time, you will succeed. But sometimes, you will fail.

🐾 When one animal in a multi-species family begins acting-out, that animal may be the symptom-bearer of a larger problem that involves the whole family.

🐾 Animal communicators are not veterinarians—unless, of course, they are. And it is against the law for anyone without a veterinary license to practice veterinary medicine or to dispense veterinary advice. *So don't do it!*

🐾 Animal communication, energy healing, and excellent veterinary care should work together. One doesn't replace another.

Lesson Ten: Communicating with Clients and Counseling Multispecies Families

- 🐾 A big part of the professional animal communicator's job is coming up with agreed-upon solutions that will work for everyone in a multi-species family.

- 🐾 In making life-and-death decisions, it is especially important to make sure that you are clear of agendas.

- 🐾 Relay the information you've received, then let the animal's human companion do with it what they will.

- 🐾 Maintain confidentiality; don't tell anything about your client or their animal companion that they don't expressly give you permission to share.

LESSON TEN TASKS

This week's lesson covered the practical and ethical considerations inherent in your role as a go-between in multi-species relationships.

1. Write about any tough issues that arose this week in counseling multi-species families. Did you ask yourself these questions: Is it true? Is it kind? Is it necessary?

2. Continue communicating with at least one each day. Continue making notes and validating whenever possible. Write about your experiences, your failures, and your victories. Continue meditating and taking care of yourself.

3. Begin making a list of veterinarians, animal behaviorists, holistic healers, and other animal professionals—including other communicators—that you know well enough to recommend when you aren't the expert, or aren't able to help out for another reason such as time constraints or illness.

4. Have you encountered any sticky situations with human communication that I haven't covered in this lesson? Write about the situation, how you felt about it, and whether you handled it as well as you could have.

LESSON ELEVEN: Special Challenges

This lesson drills down into some of the more difficult challenges you may encounter while communicating with animals and working with their multi-species family members.

Figure 47: Here at Dragonfly Pond Farm, everyone has to get along with everyone else. With more than a dozen species living together, respect for all other family members (and visitors!) is a must. It's the rule, and because of animal communication, everybody knows it. In this photo, Jack and Lightning are in the foreground, with Alyss in the background.

In this lesson:

🐾 We will discuss the ways in which deeply-entrenched problem behaviors develop, and how animal communication can help to solve, or at least minimize, the impact of these issues.

🐾 We will talk about managing expectations. Animal communication, with or without energy healing, can be a one-and-done deal, but in tough situations, it is more often an ongoing process.

🐾 We will discuss how animal communication can help people find lost or missing animals, and what to do when you receive information that leads you to believe the lost animal is dead.

🐾 We will touch on the subject of metaphysical phenomena you may encounter and what to do if that happens.

Lesson Eleven: Special Challenges

Helping Animals with Behavior Problems or Emotional Issues

Behavior problems and emotional issues can stem from any number of sources, often more than one, including but not limited to:

- 🐾 Ancestral patterns; inherited or projected.

- 🐾 In-utero trauma experienced by the animal or its mother.

- 🐾 Trauma or abuse.

- 🐾 Physical problems causing emotional distress.

- 🐾 Learned behaviors from other animals.

- 🐾 Poor training or leadership from human family members.

- 🐾 Situational or environmental triggers.

- 🐾 Misunderstanding over some past event.

These are only a few I've come across, and I'm sure there are more I haven't yet seen.

Usually, animals who are acting out will display a combination of behavioral and emotional issues that stem from a combination of sources. If it's just one source, a single communication and healing session might yield an overnight miracle. More often, healing comes from chipping-the-iceberg or peeling-the-onion.

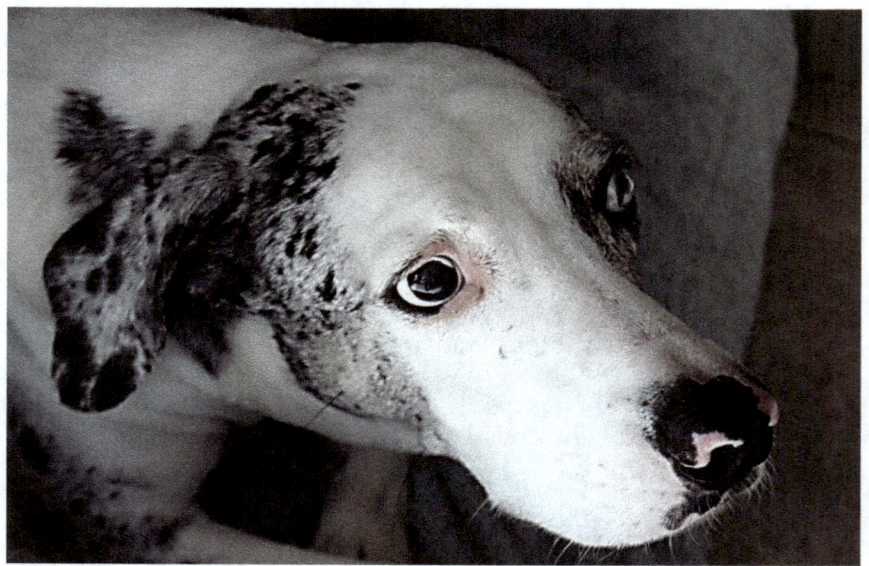

Figure 48: Truman is our special needs dog. He is deaf, has impaired eyesight, and suffers from post-traumatic stress. His right eye is black because the iris is prolapsed, probably due to abuse he suffered as a puppy. I suspect that he also has some brain damage for the same reason. Animal communication and energy healing saved his life, but he will never be a "normal" dog. Photo by Peter Berry.

Lesson Eleven: Special Challenges

Chipping the Iceberg: Truman's Story

Icebergs are much larger than they appear, because most of the mass is under the surface (subconscious or inherited, often with murky origins the animal can't tell you about). Hard as rock, icebergs are an enigma not easily cracked. Most iceberg-animals end up being euthanized, unless someone is stubborn (or stupid) enough to take them on as a cause.

Truman is a foster-failure, which means I brought him home expecting to move him on to a forever home, but it turned out that we were it. Truman was dumped at the animal shelter by someone who didn't leave a name or any background on why they'd left him there. The newly-hired staff member who took the dog in didn't ask for any contact information or background. Truman was dumped, with no name, no reason, no explanation.

On his arrival at the shelter where I volunteered, he was in such extreme fear that everything he ate went straight through him. He was rapidly losing weight to the point that the shelter staff feared for his life. My efforts of communication with Truman yielded a whole lot of silence. He was too wrapped up in his own trauma, running circles inside his paranoid mind, to communicate well. But it was clear from his trembling fear of humans that he had been badly abused.

I took him home as a foster, fully believing that a little love would set him right. I had never met an animal my magic touch couldn't transform, and I knew this dog wouldn't be any different. But I was wrong. After several months of working with Truman, I had to admit that he would never be adoptable. Because unfortunately, some icebergs are too big, or too hard, to ever be completely melted.

When I first brought Truman home as a foster dog, I gave him daily healing sessions, even spent hours sitting with him and singing lullabies when that came up as a priority under "other healing modalities." (It took quite a while, using my intuition and then validating through muscle-testing, for me to figure out what "other modality" I was supposed to use, because as you might expect, singing lullabies isn't listed in the top 100 energy healing trends.)

Months of daily healing sessions showed little progress in calming his fears. I had to go on faith that my help *was* helping. The only evidence of change was that he relaxed visibly during those lullaby-singing sessions. With little visible improvement in his level of fear the rest of the time, only my stubborn determination kept me going. I had to trust that even though the iceberg I could see above the surface wasn't changing, healing was occurring underneath, too deep for me to see.

In Truman's first few weeks with us, he was too fearful to be anywhere but a closed crate in a quiet corner of the house. His anxiety caused extreme diarrhea, even with medication. I had to take him out on a leash every two or three hours (day and night). He walked like a crab, with his back legs splayed out to the sides as if his hips were out of alignment. One day, when I watched him

Lesson Eleven: Special Challenges

walk across the yard in his awkward, shambling way, a sense of knowing gave me the first nugget of information about Truman's past: He'd been beaten so often that he'd learned to walk in a crouched position to escape notice.

Slowly, slowly, a continuous drip, drip of love and compassion began to wear away Truman's sharp edges. As his trust increased little by little, he began to reveal his past to me. I learned that he had been abused from puppyhood until the age of two, when he was finally released to the animal shelter.

I also learned from observation (and a vet exam) that he has been deaf since birth, and his vision is limited, due to inbreeding and/or repeated blows to the head. (His deficiencies in hearing and vision weren't something he could tell me about because to him, it was normal. I first confirmed his deafness by dropping a heavy kitchen pan on the floor beside him while he was sleeping. He didn't even flinch.)

In his photo, you can see that his right eye is almost completely black from a prolapsed iris, which is usually caused by trauma to the eye. His left pupil is abnormal, too, shaped like a comma instead of a circle. I also believe he has lasting brain damage from the abuse he suffered.

The deck was stacked—severely—against that dog.

Truman had been living with us for about three months before he wagged his tail. After six months, he felt confident enough to be loose in the house outside his crate. After eight months, I could trust him not to bolt if I let him outside without a leash. We had him for a year before he would voluntarily allow me to touch his body above the hips.

Truman has been my teacher in many ways. He has shown me that some scars are slow to heal, and some never will. I have learned that healing can be a slow process—and that delayed healing can be a blessing. We often learn more than we would have if we'd been granted an overnight miracle.

I've been certified as a Body Talk™ Practitioner (an energy healing modality that works for humans and animals). I'm a Reiki Master, and I know many other energy healing modalities as well. In my years of healing animals and humans, I had never encountered a case as difficult as Truman's. When I had the opportunity to consult a fellow healer while attending a conference in Colorado, I asked her to help me with Truman, who was in Alabama with my family. Using me as a surrogate, my friend performed a remote session for Truman.

During the session, I used one of the tools in my animal communication toolkit, energetically inhabiting Truman's body (after getting his permission, of course). My friend used a time-travel method to take Truman back to one of the most traumatic instances of abuse. The difference was that this time, he would have the strength and support he needed to fight back. My friend held the sacred space of protection and healing, and together we re-imagined Truman's trauma so that he could energetically win back his power.

During the reimagining and restructuring of the past event in which Truman traded his victimized persona for that of a strong and resilient survivor, my entire body trembled with reaction. I was aware of every moment, completely hooked-in to my experience, as well as the experience Truman must have had when he trembled so violently with fear that his body was completely out of his own control.

I called my husband right after the session to see if he'd noticed any change. (I certainly had!) But he reported that Truman was sleeping, and had been for the past hour, the entire time we were doing the session. Because we were in different time zones, my husband and I agreed that we would talk again in the morning.

For the rest of that evening, every light switch I touched sparked with static electricity. The next morning, my husband (who is a physicist and has to see something—like about ten times—to believe it) reported that Truman woke up "a different dog." His demeanor was more relaxed and friendly, and his crab-like shuffle had disappeared. He moved and ran more like a normal dog.

I had been a professional practitioner of energy healing and animal communication for several years by that time, but I think that was when my husband finally became a true believer. A significant chunk of Truman's iceberg had fallen away, overnight.

But that big breakthrough hadn't won the war. The iceberg's balance had shifted, rolling to reveal another facet of Truman's past that he hadn't, up until now, been able to release.

When I returned home, I noticed that Truman had gained a little weight. (With reduced anxiety, he was burning fewer calories.) I slipped my fingers under his collar to make sure it wasn't too tight, and he freaked out, jerking loose and backing away from me. I asked him why, and he showed me a picture of himself being held by the collar while someone sprayed him in the face with a water hose. At the time, he had been terrified he would drown, and any touch on his collar reignited that fear.

So many seemingly unrelated things fell into place when he showed me that picture! In that moment, I realized why he wouldn't come near the house when I ran the garden sprinklers. I realized why he would literally shit himself with fear every time we tried to give him a bath.

The minute he showed me that part of his past, I unbuckled his collar and tossed it in the trash. He watched the collar fall, then sat with a look of disbelief on his face. Then, he crept up to me and leaned against my leg, and for the first time since he'd come to us, he willingly allowed me to run my hands from the tip of his nose to the tip of his tail. That touch was so overwhelming to his system that he shuddered, and then ran a circle around the house before coming back to me for another caress. Now, that whole-body caress is something he craves and asks for regularly.

Lesson Eleven: Special Challenges

Truman is now a permanent member of the family, not because we chose him, but because he chose to stay with us. And though he may not be the easiest dog to live with, we know what an honor it is that he chose us to share his journey from fear into love.

> Some icebergs, once you've managed to break them into enough pieces, will suddenly melt away. You might be standing there with your icepick raised when you realize you've won the war. Other icebergs can be diminished, but never fully dissolved. Often, that happens because it's easier to declare a truce than it is to continue the fight.

Once Truman calmed down enough that we could all live with his Truman-ness, I was able to cut back on his energy healing sessions. With dozens of animals living at Dragonfly Pond Farm—not to mention the semi-high-maintenance animals of the human variety—I simply don't have time to give ongoing healing sessions to everyone. But with the help of daily doses of anti-anxiety medication (for him, not me) and energy healing when something goes sideways, Truman lives a happy-enough life.

Truman still isn't a normal dog. He never will be. He refuses to go outside after dark. He will only go out certain doors, from certain directions. His version of playing with the other dogs is to bowl over whoever has the ball (because he can't see the ball, but he can tell who has it). We're careful with him—though he has never bitten anyone, he will snap if he feels cornered—and if he ever needs veterinary care, I have to be "on it" with my communication and healing skills so he can withstand the stress.

As Truman's vision deteriorates, his anxiety escalates. One day, his anxiety may consume him to the point that his life is a burden to him rather than a joy. Thankfully, that is a conversation that Truman and I will be able to have. And if I'm too emotionally connected to be clear, my trusted network of animal communicator colleagues will be there to help.

Peeling the Onion

Most behavioral and emotional problems are developed one layer at a time. Perhaps the animal is born with some of the layers. Then, through bad luck, misunderstanding, poor training, or whatever, more layers are built onto the top of the core issue (or issues).

This dynamic is illustrated in the story of a puppy we'll call Rex. It is true-to-life but entirely fictional in that it doesn't represent any one dog. I've cobbled Rex's tale from many sad stories I've encountered as an animal communicator.

Figure 49: *This isn't Rex, but it is a shelter dog, who may have arrived at the shelter with misconceptions that can be uncovered and released with animal communication.*

Our fictional dog Rex has post-traumatic stress trauma along with a hereditary propensity toward anxiety. His mother's lack of nutrition when Rex was in utero gave Rex a belief system that food is scarce. These issues form the core of the onion. Then, more layers are added.

Rex is born in puppy mill, in a tiny cage. The floor of the cage is caked with his mother's urine and feces. In the wild, a mama dog will give birth to her puppies in a den she has dug out of a hill or dirt mound. She will go away from the den to hunt, eat, pee, and poo, and she will lick her puppies clean and eat their poo so the smell of their excrement won't attract predators.

But this puppy-mill mother knows that cleaning up after her babies isn't possible, when already she has to lie in her own filth. So the usual bonding process of a loving mother dog licking her puppies clean isn't part of the bonding process that Rex will experience. Because the cage is too small for the litter of growing puppies to play together, Rex will miss the developmental opportunity of learning from his siblings, too.

Rex's mom cowers at the back of her cage whenever a human approaches, so her fear of humans is projected onto him. She growls when a food bowl is slid through the cage door, so Rex learns to growl in the presence of food.

When a human reaches in with gloved hands to remove Rex's mother from the cage, she snaps. Rex learns that aggression is an appropriate reaction to fear. Because Rex's mom won't willingly be removed from her cage, the humans use a hose to spray away the filth, without first removing Rex or his siblings. Water is now added to the list of Rex's fears. More layers are added to the growing onion.

When Rex's well-meaning first-family adopts him, they are enchanted by his freshly-washed fur, his bittersweet puppy breath, his pleading brown eyes. They don't notice that he is clinging to them out of fear, not love.

When they get Rex home and put him down on the kitchen floor, his nails skitter on the bare tile—a surface he has never felt before. His first experience of his new home is frightening. He is so overwhelmed that he pees where he stands. His new family, in

Lesson Eleven: Special Challenges

their eagerness to potty-train Rex, snatch him up quickly, scold him sharply, and take him outside, where they plop him down in the grass (another surface he's never experienced) and speak to him in a demanding tone he doesn't understand, because he is too afraid to listen.

He doesn't understand what they want him to do, but he quickly learns that peeing is something he should only do when no one can see him. He goes under or behind furniture to do his business. Rex's first-family tries for four long months to potty-train him. They try swatting him with newspapers. They try shoving his nose into his excrement. They try tossing him out the back door and keeping him there until his lonely howls threaten to wake the neighbors.

In disgust, they toss him into his crate for the night, but he doesn't seem to understand that he isn't supposed to soil his bedding, so in the morning, he is dripping wet and stinky. They yell, scream, hose him down, and lock him in the garage.

Nothing works.

The next day, when he poops under a dining room chair, the frustrated woman of the house chases him into a corner and grabs him by the scruff.

He bites.

The well-meaning family feels that they've tried everything to help Rex. They would give him another chance, but they have young children, and they can't keep a dog they can't trust. At six months of age, Rex is dumped at the shelter. His cute-puppy stage is gone, and now he has three big strikes against him: food aggression, fear biting, and inappropriate peeing. What more can happen to make Rex's rehabilitation even more challenging?

Unfortunately, a lot, Rex's story is all-too common. And there are many variations on the theme. Rex's problems didn't develop overnight, and they won't be solved overnight, either. Many layers have been added to the onion, so it will take a concerted effort over time to help Rex become a happy, well-adjusted dog. And yet it could happen, if Rex is lucky enough to find a loving, well-informed human family who will be patient and compassionate during his recovery. His new family will have to enlist the support of a veterinarian, an animal communicator, an energy healer, and a behaviorist.

Let's say Rex does land in a foster home where his human rescuer has extensive knowledge of dog behavior and a support network of professionals to help.

Let's say that in Rex's peeling-the-onion situation, his first animal communication session gives him the opportunity to relay his sadness and confusion. The communicator can explain to Rex that his foster family loves him and wants to help him to heal. Rex may not be able to trust yet, but a kernel of hope has been planted.

Let's postulate that the first energy healing session addresses Rex's formative weeks of living in a dirty crate. That night, he might not pee in his crate. In his second session, his inability to bond with his siblings comes up as a priority, so in the following

Lesson Eleven: Special Challenges

days, he begins to show an interest in playing with the other dogs in the house.

His third and fourth sessions address his mother's inability to bond with him, and he begins to bond with the matriarch of the family dog pack. He starts following her when she goes outside. He begins to learn from her example that peeing and pooping outside is what's expected in this new place. The fifth and sixth sessions might clear the trauma from his first-family's abuses related to potty-training, so he stops having accidents in the house altogether.

Every healing session removes another layer of trauma. Over time, a combination of unconditional love, appropriate training, energy healing, and animal communication can help Rex become a happy, well-adjusted dog.

Communicating with Lost or Missing Animals

Communicating with lost or missing animals is a challenge. So much so that many professional animal communicators decline to work on lost or missing animal cases. It's not just because these cases are hard; it is also because they can be very upsetting. I've communicated with "lost" cats who were hit by cars, and with others who were killed by dogs. I've connected with "lost" dogs who decided to leave their home and strike out for the great unknown. How to communicate these situations to the animals' human companions is a challenge.

Another challenge is getting clear, consistent information from the lost animal. When an animal's brain has switched into fight-or-flight mode, they may not remember relevant details of where they've been. The information they give you may be out-of-order. They may have blocked or erased some particularly scary things from memory. Even when they can give a correct accounting of where they've been, what has happened to them, and where they are right now, that information may be of no value in helping to locate them.

While animal communication may not give the targeted info you would need to send out a search party, helping the lost animal to help himself is a good plan. If the animal is microchipped or wearing a collar with a contact phone number, the best way to help him get back home is to encourage him to ask a human for help.

Lesson Eleven: Special Challenges

A friend's dog ran away from her while visiting a dog park. When he saw a deer run past, he slipped under the fence in single-minded pursuit. My friend ran around to the entrance gate and followed, as right-behind-him as a human could be. She was on the phone with me within minutes. I connected with the dog, who was too focused on following the deer to chat right then, but I did get a visual of the dog veering through the forest after the deer's white-tailed rump, which got farther and farther away. Eventually, the dog lost sight of his prey, then shifted into a nose-to-ground method of pursuit.

By the time the dog slowed down enough to realize that he had possibly done a very foolish thing, he had traveled several miles. My friend and I were still on the phone, and more than an hour had passed. I asked the dog to show me an image of the landscape around him. He showed me a grassy field surrounded by evergreens. The field was bordered by a livestock fence. When I told my friend this, she got excited. "I see it! I'm walking there now."

I asked the dog how far he had gone, and he didn't have a concept of miles-traveled. He did show me a non-literal image that looked like a dart board. A central bull's eye marked the place where he had started chasing the deer. He showed himself on the outside ring of the dart board.

The message: he had traveled a very long way.

I told my friend that I had the feeling her dog had gone much farther than she could possibly follow, but she was determined.

She tried to find the landmarks I relayed, and we did this for another half-hour or so, until she hit a barrier fence that the dog wasn't showing me. This proved, finally, that while the landscape might have been similar, she and her dog were not in the same area.

She kept saying that he couldn't possibly have gone too far; the area was bordered by busy highways or bodies of water that he wouldn't be able to cross. I asked the dog again how far he had gone, and again he showed me the dart-board image, only this time, the image had an added ring around the bull's eye. I told him to stop moving, and asked if he felt that he was in a safe-enough place to spend the night.

He was tired, so he found a place to hunker down for the night. Then, my friend and I reached an agreement. She would turn back and head for home before she, too, became lost in the dark, and I would check in with her dog first thing in the morning.

When I connected with the dog the next day, he relayed a visual of the area where he had spent the night: nothing but trees and more trees. But the night before, he had passed a strip-center of shops surrounding a neighborhood of modest but well-kept homes. Though he wasn't inclined to approach people he didn't know, I convinced him to backtrack to the neighborhood and choose a house that felt safe to him. I told him to sit in front of a friendly-looking house and wait for a human to offer help.

Lesson Eleven: Special Challenges

My friend got a call twenty minutes later from a nice woman who had just returned home from taking her kids to school to find a sweet puppy sitting in front of her house as if asking for help in finding his way home.

He had traveled 28 miles in less than 24 hours.

As incredible as the scenario of a lost animal finding help in less than an hour may seem, it has happened more than once. Another lost dog (one who wasn't microchipped or wearing ID tags) found help within a half hour of a communication session. He had been missing for a couple of days, but hadn't gone more than a few miles from home, so lost dog signs were posted on every stop sign, and all he had to do was show himself to the right person.

The dog's human described a nice man who had promised to be looking out for her dog. She told me what his house looked like, and I relayed that image to the dog. Though there were probably many houses in the area matching the description, the dog found the right place. The man called her, and she and her dog were reunited in less than an hour.

These sorts of lost-animal cases are gratifying, but it isn't always that easy. In one case, a cat went missing during the first winter freeze. His human enlisted my help right away. The cat showed himself crossing the street in front of his house and going down the block along the sidewalk. He didn't have anywhere special to go; he was just strolling through the neighborhood that consisted of rows and rows of identical townhomes. I was able to track the cat as he turned right and went down another block.

He became entranced by the falling snow and stopped paying much attention to where he was going. The stubborn fall leaves that had clung to the trees were finally drifting loose to scud across the snowy surface that blanketed yards and sidewalks, and the cat was having a grand time chasing the dry leaves.

After a while, he got cold and noticed warm air coming from an open basement window. The window was half-hidden behind a line of shrubs and open just-enough for the cat to slip through. He jumped down into the basement and huddled behind a big metal cylinder that resembled a hot water heater. There were other metal boxes down there; presumably a washer and dryer.

He stayed in the basement for several hours, getting warm, taking a little siesta. Then he started getting hungry and decided it was time to go home. But the window ledge he'd easily jumped down from wasn't so easy to leap up to. He tried and tried, but couldn't make it. He cried for help until his voice was hoarse, but no one heard. All he could do was to wait for someone to come into the basement and find him.

I relayed this information to the cat's person. She put on her coat and walked street after street after street. She posted pictures of her cat on every lamppost. No one ever called. She never saw a house with an open basement window, and the cat was never found—at least, not by his human. I tried to connect with the cat again over the coming weeks, but I never got anything more. The timeline I'd been following stopped in that basement. The cat may have died there, still waiting.

While it is possible to connect with an animal's spirit after death, in this situation, I wasn't able to. Perhaps my fear of learning the truth blocked me from receiving it.

Is the Missing Animal Lost or Dead?

Tread carefully when determining whether to relay dead/not dead information to a client.

I could have concluded that the cat in the basement had died, because the picture didn't change. I didn't get a sense of "Hooray, I've been rescued!" I got a sense of waiting, waiting, waiting, and nothing changed after that.

I didn't tell the cat's person that the cat had died, because I didn't know for sure. This sort of situation definitely rates the three questions: *Is it true?* (Can you be completely sure you're right?) *Is it kind?* (Would this only upset the person or would it give them needed closure?) *Is it necessary?* (What could the human do with this knowledge that would be helpful to them or the animal?)

One of the big questions a missing animal's human wants answered is whether their animal companion is dead. They want the answer, sometimes as much as they don't want it. So be careful how you handle this sensitive matter. You could be wrong, for a variety of reasons. And you could be right, but even then, what to tell and what to hold back can be a difficult decision.

When my cousin's cat disappeared, the cat showed me a video clip of himself walking from one back yard into another, then being attacked by a dog he hadn't known was there.

The whole thing happened in an instant. The cat didn't feel any pain. He was slipping through the fence one second, and his spirit was sitting on top of it the next, watching the big dog shake his body like a stuffed toy.

Often, when an animal is blindsided by an attack or accident (such as being hit by a car) the animal's spirit will fly away at the first impact. Then the spirit will sit nearby and wait to see if the body will revive. In his case, it didn't.

I passed the vision through the three questions (true, kind, necessary) and decided to tell my cousin what I had seen. Had this been a client I didn't know well, I doubt I would have told the vision's end. Instead, I would have described the area (a wrought-iron fence under shade trees) and the possibility of a dog attack, then advised my client to ask neighbors whether they had seen anything.

I have learned, from animals, that the spirit will fly a short distance from the body after a sudden impact. I saw it happen with one of my chickens. One day, I was sitting at my desk writing, and I heard the guineas' clattering cry of alarm. I rushed outside to see that a red-tailed hawk had my little black hen pinned to the ground, and the guineas were raising holy hell

Lesson Eleven: Special Challenges

about it. I shooed the hawk away from the hen (I recognize that hawks have to eat, too, but not when I'm around).

My little black hen looked dead. Completely limp, eyes closed. I couldn't tell if she was breathing. If she was, it was very shallow. But there wasn't a mark on her body. It occurred to me that her spirit may be nearby, waiting for the all-clear signal before reinhabiting the body. I put her limp body in a nest box inside the chicken coop and closed the door. After an hour, I went back and opened the coop door. She hopped out, shook out her feathers, and went on about her business, scratching for worms in the chicken yard.

Figure 50: *This little black hen was attacked by a hawk when she was out foraging. I thought she was dead, and so did she, but it turned out that she wasn't.*

Then there's the opposite side of the coin. Some animals don't yet realize they're dead (and this may have been why I didn't get any further information from the cat waiting to be found in the basement).

This happens more frequently than you'd think. The story I'm about to tell isn't a missing-animal case, but it does pertain to the dead/not dead question.

A client called me one evening, crying because she'd come home from work to find her young dog dead in the back yard. The dog, Allie, was lying in the yard as if sleeping, with no signs of injury. My client wanted me to connect with Allie's spirit and ask what had caused her death.

I connected in with Allie and asked what had killed her. Her surprised response: "Dead? I'm dead? Well, that explains everything! No wonder I couldn't wake up from my nap! No wonder everyone's crying! Oh, my goodness, I'm dead!"

That answered the question; Allie had died in her sleep. I continued the conversation, asking Allie if she wanted to reincarnate anytime soon, and got an immediate and enthusiastic, "Yes, right away!" I asked what she'd come back as, and she said she would come back as a cat. When I told my client that, she laughed through her tears. "Of course she would. Because we always called her Allie Cat."

It is possible to communicate with animals who are no longer in their physical body. The process of connecting-in is the same as working remotely with a live animal. Some of the questions will be the same, but many will differ. Here are some ideas for good questions to ask animals in spirit:

- Where is your spirit now?

- What is it like there?

- Do you forgive me for ____(any baggage or unfinished business)____?

- Were you ready to transcend when you did?

- Are you planning to reincarnate anytime soon?

- If you do reincarnate, will you come back as the same kind of animal, or something different?

- Will you reincarnate to be with me again? Or will you have a new life-mission to be with someone else?

- Are you in communication with ____(anyone they knew who has also passed)____?

Animals in spirit can be an incredible source of information on the workings of the universe. Ask an animal anything you're curious about; they may be able to enlighten you.

Spirits and Otherworldly Concerns

Figure 51: *You may not believe in ghosts, but Georgia does. I don't have the ability to see ghosts, but Georgia does. Once, when I saw her growling at something in the forest behind our house, I asked what she was looking at. She showed me a group of gray, tattered-looking men in civil-war uniforms, trudging through the forest. I called a friend who is adept at mediumship. She validated Georgia's visions and made a house call to help the lost soldiers find their way to the light.*

As I have hinted—and glossed-over so far—there are things in this world that we cannot begin to understand, and you may run across some of them while doing the work of animal

Lesson Eleven: Special Challenges

communication. I would be remiss if I didn't tell you at least a little about some of the things you may encounter.

You don't need to worry, because you know how to center, ground, and protect yourself. But the ignorant or unaware among us may need our guidance, and that is why I include this information.

It is easy for animals (and humans) to unwittingly invite-in energies outside themselves in times of despair or distress. In the case of humans, it can also happen because of ignorance, arrogance, or sheer stupidity.

I once had an interesting communication session with a cat during a psychic fair. The cat wasn't present, but the cat's person—a young woman—had brought a photo, so we worked from that. She didn't have any questions or concerns; she just wanted to know what her cat had to say, if anything.

I kept seeing an image of the woman sitting in a chair, hunched over a notebook, writing with a pencil. The cat was sitting under the chair, projecting a feeling of unease and worry. He felt that the woman was doing something very dangerous, and he was trying to maintain a protective shield around the woman.

When I relayed this picture to the woman, she insisted that she never wrote with a pencil. She was going to college, but she took all her notes on the computer. I reconnected with the cat for validation, and again got the same picture, along with the same feeling of danger.

It took some back-and-forth conversation before the woman finally remembered that she used a pencil for drawing. She was taking an art class, and one of the requirements of the class was to fill a sketchbook with drawings. She hadn't snapped to my meaning because I had used the word "writing" instead of "drawing." (Notice that while I had received the picture correctly, I had misinterpreted a key element. This kept the woman from immediately understanding the intended message.)

To find out what was going on that the cat found so threatening, I asked the woman to describe her creative process. She told me that she had recently become interested in all things metaphysical, so she had developed a practice of going into a meditative state, then inviting any spirits who might be hanging around to help her in the creation of her art.

Inviting spirits or ghosts or otherworldly beings to "Come on in!" is a bad idea, and the cat knew that even if the woman didn't.

The woman and I had a little talk about boundaries and protection, and I did some energy healing to help move along any unwanted energies she may have unwittingly invited into her home.

You may encounter humans or animals who are troubled by ghosts or other energies. You can sometimes see the shadows or orbs of spirits in photos provided to you for communication purposes. Moving these energies safely on to their next right place is beyond the scope of this book, but knowing that they exist, you can at least be prepared to discuss the subject if it comes up in a telepathic conversation. If you aren't trained to help these energies move on, refer your client to someone who is. (There are resources on my website, www.HearThemSpeak.com.)

"You're **not from around here, are** you?"

One of the most freaky (and fun!) things about animal communication is when you meet an animal who seems to hail from another planet, another universe, or another dimension.

Reincarnation is common, and people are often aware that their new puppy seems eerily similar in appearance and mannerisms to a dog they once had. Those people usually understand why that is. But less-often, you'll meet animals who just aren't like everyone else.

Take, for example, the octopus.

I had heard Jack Rudloe talk about the strange ability of octopus to connect psychically with humans. And as the president of Gulf Specimen Marine Lab—which supplies marine organisms to schools and research laboratories, and serves as an environmental education center for the Florida Panhandle—Jack is in a position to know.

Jack has also written eight nationally published non-fiction books, as well as articles for many magazines, including National Geographic, Smithsonian, Natural History, and Audubon.

He is, quite simply, an expert on marine life.

In describing his octopus encounters, Jack had used words like sinister and disturbing, a feeling that when the octopus wraps its tentacles around your hand, it's somehow attempting to "suck your soul."

I was skeptical. Not because I don't believe in the psychic abilities of animals. In fact, I do believe. I was skeptical of Jack's story because I couldn't imagine that any species could be intrinsically sinister. To describe an entire species as soul-sucking seemed a bit hyperbolic.

In my experience, most animals are incredibly similar to humans in their thought processes, their dreams, and their daily concerns. They care about the people and animals they love and think of as family. They care about their environment and their home. They have hopes and wishes and worries. Many have lofty life missions, while others are more concerned with comfort and enrichment.

How could an octopus be so different?

Admittedly, most of my communications have been with animals who live with people. I converse with mammals, birds, and the occasional reptile. There hasn't been much need for my services in the ocean environment. So when Jack offered me the opportunity to experience the sinister way an octopus has of sucking your soul, I pounced!

At the Marine Lab, I dipped my hand into the cold water of the octopus tank and connected telepathically with the closest octopus. I initiated the communication the way I always do, sending a thought-message of greeting. The octopus didn't answer, but she blushed, just a little, before coyly sliding away from me and settling in a different area of the tank. Her telepathic message: "I don't know you. You smell funny."

Jack and I talked a bit about the ability of an octopus to smell underwater. I greeted another octopus in the tank, one who was still feeling uncomfortable in his new environment. I sent some healing energy to help him acclimate.

Then I tried again with the shy girl who'd spurned my advances. This time, when I dangled my hand in the water, she reached up with one tentacle and walked it gently up my wrist. Accustomed to my funny smell by then, she wrapped her tentacle around my arm. Then, she began exploring with a second tentacle. With each little suction cup, she tugged insistently, pulling my arm farther into the tank with surprising force.

"What do you want?" I asked.

"More," she answered. "Come in." Her voice in my head sounded soft and compelling, a siren's call that promised the world to me if I'd obey her command. She wanted me to come into the water, not just my arm, but my whole self. She showed an image of what she wanted to do: explore my human form with her tentacles so she could learn more about humans in general, and me in particular. The fact that I wouldn't be able to breathe underwater didn't concern her.

I have been lucky enough to commune with many different animals. I've stared into an ocelot's eyes in mutual meditation, receiving a silent download of ancient information, deeper than words, deeper even than feeling and emotion. I've been thoroughly sniffed by dogs and cats who wanted to know more about me and where I've been. But this octopus wanted more than just to know me.

She wanted to become me.

She wanted to devour the essence of my humanness and take it into herself. Like the Borg from Start Trek, she wanted to assimilate me. I understood now what Jack meant about an octopus sucking your soul. This was no mutual meditation. This was purely about her taking something of me into herself, with no plan of giving anything in return.

While she held my arm, I felt a definite flow of information energy being funneled into her consciousness. With all those voracious little suction cups, she was probing my mind through my skin, doing her own version of the Vulcan mind-meld. I felt like a human subject who'd been beamed into an alien mother ship.

Perhaps octopuses aren't animals, after all. Maybe they're little aliens sent down here to learn about the human race. For what purpose? I don't know. Maybe nothing sinister after all, but it is a little unnerving to have one's inner landscape explored with such intensity.

When she had dragged my arm so far into the water that the short sleeve of my shirt was getting wet, I pulled back, allowing her a less intense connection, just giving her my fingers. With

Lesson Eleven: Special Challenges

only a few of her suction cups gently massaging my fingers, I asked her telepathically if there was anything she wanted to tell me. She showed me an image of a hideaway under a shelf rock—the home she remembered from the open sea. When I told this to Jack, he immediately gave instructions for one of the interns to find a flat rock and construct a shelter for her as it had been described.

I asked the octopus if she had a name. Her tentacles probed my hand (and my mind) for a moment, then came up with the name of a character in a book I'm writing. Olivia.

I asked Olivia if she had any questions for me. She wanted to know why she had been brought to the Marine Lab, and how long she would be staying. I explained that she would stay for the rest of her life so that she could learn about people, and people could learn about her. Her suction cups pulsed against my fingers for a moment, as if she was thinking about the idea. She let me understand that her intellectual mode is one of exploration, not exposition. Of learning, not teaching. Of receiving, not giving.

"But Olivia," I thought to her. "You are giving, even though you don't realize it. You've given me the experience of your touch. You aren't as reticent as you think. You've let me into your mind, too, if only a little. What if you decided to do it consciously? You could be a great teacher, if you wanted to."

"I'll think about it," she replied. Then she released my fingers and gently pushed my hand away.

LESSON ELEVEN HIGHLIGHTS

🐾 This lesson covered some of the more difficult challenges you may encounter while communicating with animals and working with their multi-species family members.

🐾 Animal communication can help to solve, or at least minimize, the impact of problem behaviors that developed over time. Healing from trauma can be a one-and-done deal, but in tough situations, it is more often an ongoing process.

🐾 Lost or missing animals are difficult to locate through telepathy alone, because often the animal is too fearful and stressed-out to be a good communicator. Even when a lost animal can communicate well, the information they impart may not be helpful in locating them. Giving good advice to a lost animal (stop running, ask for help) is often more successful than trying to pinpoint their location.

🐾 Be mindful when deciding what to tell an animal's human companion when you receive information that leads you to believe the animal is dead.

🐾 You may encounter animals who are troubled by ghosts or other energies. If this happens and you aren't trained to deal with this situation, refer your client to someone who is.

Lesson Eleven: Special Challenges

LESSON ELEVEN TASKS

1. Write about any especially tough behavioral situations you have encountered so far in this course. How did you handle them?

2. Flip back through your animal communication notebook and pick out a few of the sessions you weren't happy with. Reconnect with those animals and try again. Ask some of the same questions you asked before, but also ask a few different questions.

3. Compare the first sessions in your notebook to subsequent sessions. Ask yourself:

    a. How has your ability changed over time?

    b. What blocks did you have at the beginning that you don't have now?

    c. Are there any lingering blocks you still have to deal with? What are they?

4. Have you encountered anything "otherworldly" yet? Yes, no, maybe so?

5. Did any of this week's material about spirits or the afterlife of animals challenge your belief system? Can you open your mind to these new ideas?

6. Can you come up with an alternate explanation for the more "out there" things you aren't ready to consider?

7. Now that you are almost done with the course, write about your experiences. Did you encounter anything surprising? Witness any miracles?

8. Have you changed as a result of taking this course?

9. Has your relationship with your own animal companions changed?

LESSON TWELVE: Own Your Superpowers

In this final lesson, we will discuss how to take your new superpowers out into the world as you continue to practice and grow as a communicator. We'll also look at some tools you might want to add to your toolkit. Are you excited? I am! We're about to take off the training wheels!

Figure 52: *Small creatures are easily overlooked if you're not paying attention, but they can provide a valuable viewpoint if you take the time to notice them and listen to the wisdom they have to share.*

Remember the Importance of Boundaries

As you continue to practice and improve your skills even further, you will be invited to do some pretty cool things. If you have a burning desire to bury your face in a lion's mane, you will probably get that opportunity. I have kissed an ocelot, hugged a wolf, and petted lions and tigers. But I took the direction of expert handlers who were present and followed appropriate safety precautions, and I was careful to be fully present and aware every moment.

When exciting opportunities like these present themselves, remember that physical proximity is an important boundary. If you decide to cross it, please make sure you know what you are doing.

It is tempting to think your superpowers will allow you to approach any animal, no matter how wild, but that would be a mistake. The ability to communicate with animals doesn't come with an entitlement to be stupid without paying the consequences. Use common sense. Ask yourself whether it's necessary for you to get close enough to touch. In general, the answer is no, it's not.

When I communicated with a copperhead snake in my garden, I kept my distance. The day before writing this, I encountered a coiled water moccasin who was agitated enough to "rattle" his tail like a rattlesnake. I communicated with him by exiting the vicinity with adrenaline-fueled speed. In fact, we both skedaddled. (Our mutual message: I won't hurt you if you won't hurt me. I just want to be left alone to go about my business.)

Every action has a potential consequence. When you are offered the possibility of proximity with an animal you don't know, ask yourself whether the risk is worth taking. If the answer is yes, be mindful that you're taking a risk not only for yourself, but for the animal. If something goes wrong, they may pay a much higher price than you.

Consider Adding Energy Healing to Your Toolkit

I encourage you to explore and learn a few methods of energy healing that appeal to you. Other helpful courses are psychology, counseling, and physiology. You can probably think of many more. What learning opportunity makes you feel excited? Find and follow that path.

Animal communication is a healing modality in itself. Simply being heard and understood can work miracles. It helps when an animal is also able to understand, for the first time, what humans want and expect.

But sometimes, understanding only opens the closet door. Dragging out and unpacking all the baggage in the closet can take more effort. In these cases, energy healing adds more possibility for even greater depths of healing.

Figure 53: *Energy healing can, among other things, help animals get along in a multi-species household. These are three of our twelve cats; left-right: Teddy, Max, and Blue. (Yes, I know twelve is a lot, but we have eight acres, plenty of room for all the critters and humans to spread out.) Everyone gets along with everyone else here, because that's the rule, and everybody knows it.*

I first learned Reiki I and Reiki II. Then, over the next several years, I learned Body Talk™ and became a certified practitioner. After that, I learned Matrix Energetics (a powerful yet playful healing modality) in a week-long seminar. Since then, I have become a Reiki Master, learned to use the healing frequency of crystals and sound, learned the power of shamanic healing and angelic assistance... and... and... and. Now, I use a combination of all these modalities, and over time, some of my own techniques have begun to emerge as well.

My toolkit is always growing. Even though I have witnessed miracles arising from simple understanding and the most basic healing modalities, I continue to learn and grow as a communicator and healing practitioner. When a class that appeals to me presents itself, I take it. I recognize that I can always learn something more. I learn from animals and from my human clients. And now that I am teaching, I learn from my students. Everyone has valuable insights to share, if we are willing to learn.

It is important to continue learning and adding to your personal toolkit. Professionals in most fields are required to take continuing education courses. It keeps them sharp and on top of their game. Always strive to deepen your knowledge and raise your skill level. Not just through practice, but through classes, networking, and learning from your peers whenever the opportunity arises.

🐾 While you are adding to your toolkit, don't forget the basics.

Listening is the foundation of what we do as animal communicators. One of the most powerful ways to help an animal heal from trauma or abuse is to sit with them and listen. First, let them tell their story, without trying to talk them out of their fears or reframing the situation. Listen with compassion and understanding. Listen completely, and let them know they've been heard.

Then, offer to help the animal reimagine the abusive or stressful situation so they will have the opportunity to rewrite that history the way my friend and I did with Truman.

Communicate with the animal and work together with him to come up with an agenda and set an intention. Call in angelic assistance if that's appropriate. Connect with the animal and reimagine the event in a way that allows him to take back his power. Imagine that you're there with him to give support and help him find the strength to reclaim the fragments of his soul that were lost or rejected in order to survive the ordeal.

As you continue to learn and grow as a communicator, your superpowers will increase, and the miracles you are able to command will surprise you. But as you increase your power, please remember that your humility should grow along with it. An overinflated ego can keep you from seeing what's right in front of you.

You may be the greatest communicator and healer that ever lived, but that doesn't mean every animal you come across will want your help. Always ask permission before getting involved, and keep checking in to ensure that you still have permission along the way. Only go where you're invited. Even if an animal gives you permission to send healing energy on Monday, by Tuesday you may have hit a layer of resistance that isn't ready to dissolve. In fact, resistance is most likely to occur after a major

Lesson Twelve: Own Your Superpowers

breakthrough. Whether you are communicating, healing, or a little of both, proceed with mindfulness and respect.

It's important to remember that healing energy can often be felt by the animal receiving it. It can feel to them like a subtle shifting of energy (similar to bubbles in your stomach after you've had a fizzy drink). It can feel hot, or cold, or tingly, or like nothing at all. The feeling may not be the same from one session to another, or even within one session.

Even subtle energy shifts can be alarming to a traumatized animal.

Be aware that your own energy may also be projected while you are sending healing. The goal is to be the conduit, not the source, but it is always possible that you could be leaking some of your own energy by mistake, and your human energy may not feel comfortable to a wary animal who has been on the receiving end of a human's bad intentions. So when you are sending healing energy, always remain attuned to your own energy projection as well as to the animal's subtle reactions. If you don't know the animal well, send the healing from a distance rather than through physical touch.

The Future Begins Now, but...

Now that you are nearing the end of this course, you may be feeling a surge of optimism and energy. You may have surprised yourself and others with the accuracy and specificity of your readings.

But please don't "hang out a shingle" until you have done literally hundreds of communications and are getting consistent validation from the people whose animals you're communicating with. I didn't start charging money until I was getting spot-on information 99 percent of the time, and I had more requests for communication than I had time to oblige.

Begin by telling friends and family that you are practicing and learning animal communication, and ask if they will allow you to communicate with their animal companions.

When you have exhausted that resource, ask your friends and family to reach out to their friends and family. Work with your own animals, asking the same questions over again, and asking different questions that come up over time. Your animal companions will be happy to help you grow in your abilities.

Working with the same animals repeatedly, asking new questions or following up on old ones, will also allow you to deepen your relationship with those animals and learn more about yourself and your abilities in the process.

You're not an expert until you are, and even then, you're not infallible. If you start billing yourself as a professional animal communicator before you are consistently accurate, you will discredit yourself and give the whole profession a bad reputation.

Don't do that to yourself. Like Mama said, you only have one chance to make a good first-impression.

Lesson Twelve: Own Your Superpowers

Begin by Volunteering

One way to get more practice is to volunteer at animal shelters. Anyone who wants to be an animal communicator should do this as part of their training. It lets you practice focus in a chaotic environment. It lets you practice getting through to animals who have their shields up. It lets you practice getting past your own shields. We automatically put up a psychic shield when we are in an emotionally chaotic environment. You may find that you have a hard time connecting, at first, in a shelter environment because of this.

If that happens, don't worry. Just keep coming back until you get used to the energy of the place. Sit outside in your car for a while before going inside. Take some time to center and ground yourself. When you have created a space of calm emptiness inside you, go inside and see what happens.

It is best to keep a physical distance when communicating with animals in shelters. Many animals in shelters are so starved for attention that their physical need to cuddle and leap about takes precedence over their desire and ability to communicate telepathically. You will get a much clearer signal if the animal isn't in your lap or climbing on you.

Animals in shelters can be anxious and reactive because of the chaotic environment and the trauma they have undergone. If you get bitten by a dog in the shelter, that dog will be euthanized.

🐾 Safety-first is important for you and for them.

Let's assume you want to talk with a dog in the shelter. If you have the advantage of a shelter employee's help, you can ask them to leash the dog and bring it into a quiet space where they can hold the dog's leash while you communicate from a short distance.

If you don't have that advantage, you will have to sit outside the dog's enclosure. Depending on the way the shelter is constructed, you may be able to sit back a bit with a view of several enclosures, and then you will have the opportunity to communicate with any dogs who are calm and willing.

Animals in the shelter environment may be feeling fearful, anxious, exited, grieving, despondent, jealous, defensive, etc. Others will be emotionally shut-down because of the trauma they've experienced. They may be closed-off to protect themselves from the barrage of emotions projected by the other animals and too much sensory input resulting from the shelter's operations: cleaning, feeding, dogs brought in and taken out, people coming and going, with or without an animal by their side.

Sometimes it helps to give energy healing—from a distance—for an animal before communicating. That will help them to relax and settle down, and it will also help you to establish a connection. If you don't yet have energy healing skills, simply sit quietly with the animal and commune with them. Allow them time to get used to your energy before you begin.

Lesson Twelve: Own Your Superpowers

Working with shelter animals will help you to hone your skills, and it will also help the animals more than you can imagine. Your time and talent can save many lives by helping animals to understand what is happening to them and why, so they can release their fears and mistaken assumptions, and connect with potential families.

Figure 54: *Volunteering at your local animal shelter can help you hone your skills. And while you are practicing, you have the opportunity to improve the life of every animal you meet.*

Shelter animals often don't realize why they are there. They wonder whether they did something wrong. Many hope that their human family is coming back to get them. They don't know if they're on death-row, or if they have time to connect with someone who might be willing to give them a home. (Some shelter animals do understand that they're living on borrowed time.)

When you volunteer, have a shelter employee walk you through the building and tell you any background information they know about each animal. That knowledge will allow you to answer any questions the animals might ask. You can explain why they were surrendered to the shelter and assure them that it wasn't their fault. You can help them release at least some of their anguish.

Shelter animals often feel a great deal of grief for the life they've lost, and guilt over anything they might have done wrong, even if they don't know what that was. And on top of all that, they are burdened by an overwhelming sense of failure. Often, these emotions will prevent them from bonding with a new or potential family, thus continuing the cycle of loss and abandonment. Your ability to communicate with an animal and clear these embedded emotions may mean the difference between life and death for them.

🐾 Animals can carry past trauma into their new lives.

I spoke with a dog whose human, Daike, was concerned that even two years after being adopted, the dog had never seemed to bond with her. The communication was done remotely, using a photograph, at a psychic fair. The dog, Astrid, felt an

Lesson Twelve: Own Your Superpowers

overwhelming sense of guilt. She had failed to protect her beloved human, and because of that, she'd been sent to live with someone else. Daike didn't know how that could be. Astrid had been only six months old when Daike adopted her from the family in which she was born.

I checked back in with Astrid for more information. She told me that she had bonded with one of the family's several children. The other puppies had all been given away, but she'd been allowed to stay, and the child she loved had promised she'd be able to stay forever. In return, she had promised to always protect the child.

The memory of this mutual promise got tangled up with circumstances to make Astrid think she had been banished from her home in disgrace.

The child fell and skinned her knee while playing in the yard, and the next day, Astrid was taken to live with Daike. Astrid linked the two events in her mind—the child falling and injuring herself, and Astrid's banishment from the family.

As humans, we are able to suppose that the two events were unlikely to be related. Maybe the adults in the family had never meant to keep Astrid, at all, but it had taken a while for them to find her a home.

Astrid was trying to make sense of the incomprehensible and had come to a wrong conclusion that kept her locked in grief and guilt. Those toxic emotions, along with a pervasive sense of failure, had kept her from bonding with her new family.

I explained to Astrid that she had done nothing wrong, and I did a remote healing session to help her release any vestiges of those stuck emotions.

The next day, I received an email from Daike.

She wrote: *I AM BEYOND words to express the IMMEDIATE change when I got home. The CHANGE extraordinary-it was/is a beautiful transition and I'm in awe of your work! Thank you! Thank you! Thank you!*

Figure 55: *This is Astrid, whose sense of guilt kept her from bonding with her new family. Now, Astrid has a happy life and a deep bond with her people - human, canine and feline! Photo by Daike Klement.*

Lesson Twelve: Own Your Superpowers

Many shelter animals have created a story to explain to themselves why they were left at the shelter. You can help them to release those toxic stories and emotions so that they are able to move on and find loving forever homes. When you've explained what happened and why, ask the animal what kind of family they'd like to have. This information can help the shelter workers to direct people to the right animal companion for them. Then, encourage the animals to "call their people." Show them how they can visualize, manifest, dream of the family and home they'd like to have, then put out a beacon to attract those people to them.

When I volunteered at the shelter, I told all the animals to call their people, every day. On a regular basis, people would come into the shelter and say something like, "I always drive past without stopping, but I felt an overwhelming compulsion to come here today." And then, they'd walk out with a newly adopted family member.

🐾 If you can communicate effectively with animals in the shelter environment, you can communicate anywhere.

When you have been practicing for a while at shelters, and with the animals of your friends and relatives and their friends and relatives, word of mouth will spread. At some point, you will find that you have more requests for communication than you have time to honor.

When that happens, it will be time for you to start branching out.

Taking It to the Next Level

If you want to explore the idea of helping others by offering your services as an animal communicator to others, public events like psychic fairs, shelter fundraisers, dog shows, agility trials, etc., are a good place to start.

You will want to have plenty of shelter experience before you try this, because these events are usually loud and chaotic and full of distractions. Also, you will be interacting with the animal's human as well as the animal. These added elements will raise the level of difficulty.

If you know another communicator you trust, you may decide to work as a team and share the expenses. In the beginning, rather than charging a fee, I suggest asking for a love offering. Another way to do this is to give a range of prices and allow clients to pay what feels comfortable for them. Or, charge a fee but donate the proceeds to your favorite animal charity. People who wouldn't normally stop by your booth will give animal communication a whirl if they know the money they spend will help animals in the community.

Lesson Twelve: Own Your Superpowers

For a number of reasons (like chipping-the-iceberg and peeling-the-onion) I offer packages of several energy healing sessions at a discount, to help people consider the long view of healing. I encourage you to do this as well.

Problems usually don't crop up overnight, and they aren't always solved that quickly, either. That's why it's good to offer ongoing sessions. But I also like to tell people to take a break after a month or so, and see how the current trajectory plays out. Because sometimes, when you have addressed the core issue and pointed the animal or family organism in the right direction, events will unfold and the universe will conspire to support the eventual evolution of the situation. And if progress stalls out, they can always call back.

I used to joke that my main goal was to put myself out of business—to fix each situation so completely that each client would never have to call me again. But situations evolve. Animal companions die, and new ones arrive. So the truth is that you won't be putting yourself out of business, no matter how good you are at problem-solving. Old clients will keep coming back, and they will refer your services to others. Sooner than you think, you'll be busier than you'd like.

Changing the Rules, Just a Little

Now that you are becoming more proficient at animal communication, it is fine if you want to get more information from an animal's companion before you connect with the animal.

When you first started practicing, I recommended that you ask an animal's human companion for as little information as possible, so you wouldn't go into a session with preconceived notions. But when you get ready to start working with clients, you will want to get more information before beginning a session.

There are two reasons for this: Time and money. Once you are sure of your abilities and know that you will be able to set-aside any information you have been given before you speak with an animal, having a framework of information will help to direct your line of questioning and make sure that you are covering your client's areas of concern. It will save you time, and once you start charging for your time, it will save your clients money.

You know from your practice that you don't have to have a photo image of the animal you are communicating with to be fully connected when doing a remote session. But having a photo can save time, and it may give additional observation information that you can set aside, but also use to direct the conversation. Facial expressions, body language, even the background in the photo can give you clues that you might want to follow up on, but they can also be misleading if you allow yourself to be influenced by appearances.

Lesson Twelve: Own Your Superpowers

Observation: a Blessing and a Curse

What you can see with your eyes can reveal a part of the puzzle you are working to solve. It's not telepathy, so I only mentioned it briefly when we first covered visual information. I wanted you to take a shot at experiencing visual telepathic information before introducing simple visual observation as something that should also be in your toolkit.

It isn't telepathy, but it is information, maybe to be set aside for later—or maybe to prompt a question you hadn't thought to ask. What you observe in the animal's environment or the behavior of that animal or its human companion(s) can add another important layer of meaning that can be useful, as long as…

…you know the difference between what you observe and what is being related to you from an animal.

…your observations aren't obscuring your ability to understand what the animal wants you to know.

…you are clear in relaying to the human client what you're getting from telepathy, and what you're getting from simple observation.

🐾 Use observation as a tool to direct the conversation, but don't prejudge the answer you might receive because of it.

Using observation can be helpful, but it can also trip you up. Be careful not to "judge a book by its cover," especially when you're working from photographs.

Basset Hounds, Blood Hounds, Clumber Spaniels, and other breeds with droopy eyes and jowls might, at first glance, look sad. Salukis and Scottish Deerhounds, Greyhounds and Whippets, with their long noses and slightly hunched-looking body shapes, can look timid and afraid. Mastiffs, Basenjis, and English Bulldogs, with their wrinkled foreheads, can look worried. I could go on and on, but you get the picture (pun intended).

Some dogs refuse to look at the camera, and the resulting photo can make them look guilty when they're not. They're simply following one rule of dog behavior: Looking straight into someone's eyes, for a dog, can be considered a challenge of authority. Some dogs are very aware of the camera as an "eye," and they won't look into it because they don't want to challenge the authority of the person holding the camera.

Injuries, illnesses, and birth defects can change an animal's appearance in a way that might give the impression of pain or discomfort where there is none—or where the pain and discomfort is something the animal simply accepts as normal. Animals don't tend to dwell on the past, cast blame on others, or

Lesson Twelve: Own Your Superpowers

feel sorry for themselves the way people do. You might ask a clearly-crippled animal who's been permanently disfigured by abuse whether they suffer from any physical problems, and they're more likely to answer no than yes.

I once asked a rescued ocelot whether he had any physical issues that needed to be addressed, and his response was, "No problems here! I love my life! So glad to be alive!"

This was his attitude, even though he had to drag his back legs behind him because he had been so severely beaten in the past.

Figure 56: *Boots had a droopy ear, and he felt bad. Both conditions are easy to see from this photo (look at his eyes; he is in pain). But anyone who combined these two separate observations to equal one conclusion would be wrong. And jumping to an erroneous conclusion from a simple observation (or an observation-tainted communication) would deprive Boots and his loving human companion of the opportunity to discover the real problem. Photo by Kevin Wattier.*

Using a photograph, I spoke with a new client's cat, Boots, who had one droopy ear. I wasn't told anything about the ear, so I didn't know whether Boots had an ear infection or some other problem that was causing him pain. But I asked if his ear bothered him, and he said no. So I moved on with the conversation.

Boots did feel bad; that was why his person, Kevin, had contacted me. And from the photo I'd been given, Boot's discomfort was easy to observe. But it didn't have anything to do with his droopy ear. The pain Boots was experiencing stemmed from kidney failure, and knowing what it was helped Kevin and the family's veterinarian to solve the problem.

When I later spoke with Kevin, I asked about the droopy ear, and was told that several years ago Boots had developed a hematoma (a solid mass of clotted blood in the tissues) that was operated on twice. While the problem was solved, the ear drooped forever after. If I had focused on appearances, I might have gotten hung up on that droopy ear and missed the point entirely.

The onset of kidney failure might have spelled the end for an old cat whose human couldn't be bothered. But with Kevin's commitment to keeping Boots healthy and happy, along with accurate animal communication, energy healing, and excellent veterinary care, the cat's life was extended by years. He lived the rest of his life in comfort and security and love until he was ready to go. And after Boots told Kevin he was ready to be helped across the Rainbow Bridge, Kevin was right beside him, taking strength from the knowledge that together, they'd made the right decision.

Tumors can cause alarming-looking disfigurations that may be ultimately fatal, but don't cause pain in the short-term. I communicated with one dog whose tumor caused a large, disfiguring lump in his face, and another whose eye appeared to be popping out because of the pressure exerted by the internal tumor.

In both these cases, I asked if the tumors hurt. Surprisingly (to me) both dogs said no. They each said that they still had work to do on this earth. Neither was ready to die or to be assisted in crossing the Rainbow Bridge. Each dog gave specific symptoms that would indicate their readiness to go, and I kept in touch with their human companions so that together we could provide support, healing, and understanding for the animal until it was time to assist in their transformation into pure spirit.

Veterinarians are happy to help when obviously sick animals are ready to transcend. But they often get a little judgmental when a healthy looking animal is done with this life and ready to move on, and this happens more often than you might think. Plenty of animals look perfectly fine on the outside, but something inside is terribly wrong, or they are just tired of soldiering on.

Physically, mentally, or emotionally, they are suffering and crying out for help. They just want to be released. And if you aren't willing to help them, they will find a way to help themselves.

> 🐾 **If you won't help an animal's wishes be heard, they will do what they have to do without your help, even though it will cause them to suffer.**

Dogs will start fights with bigger dogs who are sure to win.

Cats will climb into the inner workings of a vehicle and wait for someone to start the engine.

Horses will get themselves tangled-up in barbed wire and injured to such a degree that they have to be euthanized.

I have seen all these things and more. I am sorry to have to admit that despite our superpowers, animal communicators—and humans in general—don't know everything. Observation can provide one piece of the puzzle. Intuition, psychic abilities, and telepathy can provide more pieces. But even all of that together won't always give us everything we need to know.

If we're lucky, it'll give us enough.

So, while you should definitely use observation when something catches your attention, please don't jump to conclusions or rule-out anything based on those observations. Observations are just one piece of the puzzle that can be helpful, but can also be misleading. Notice whatever catches your attention about the situation, the environment, relationships, or any other peripheral information that offers itself up. Then use that information to guide your intuition to ask the right questions.

Figure 57: *This young, beautiful, perfectly healthy shelter dog was tired of life, tired of being disappointed by the people she had been foolish enough to trust. She was done, finished; ready to leave this life and start over again. She reminded me so much of a dog I had known and loved, though they looked nothing alike. I promised her that I would adopt her as soon as I returned from a week-long writing retreat. I promised I would come and get her, and I tried to connect with her telepathically every day, but I kept seeing an image of her looking away from me, gazing over a distant horizon. She wasn't at all interested in trusting anyone again, ever. Still, I called the shelter and told them to save her for me. I told them when I would pick her up. But before that could happen, she—this completely gentle spirit—got into a fight with a bigger dog. She was euthanized the day before I was scheduled to bring her home.*

Create a Network of Animal Communicators and Healers

Get to know other communicators and healers in your area. You will find that most are willing to share information and mentor newbies. I'm not suggesting that you make cold-calls, but as you start getting out in the world and practicing, or taking classes, you will meet others in the animal communication community. When you do, be friendly. Exchange contact information. And be sure to give as much as you get; don't ask someone to help you without giving something in return. Let them know when you hear of a new venue, such as a health-and-wellness fair, or an animal-welfare fundraiser. Share what you know. There is room-enough for everyone.

My students regularly text me with cool things they have found of interest, like links to free advertising sites for animal communicators. Because they are doing the work of reaching out to me in a positive way, I'm happy to reciprocate when I can help them.

You will one day be in a position to teach or mentor others, and when that day comes, remember how others have helped you, and do your part to grow the animal communication community. I look forward to the day when animal communication isn't seen as a fuzzy-woo-woo act performed by gypsies and vagabonds, but as a normal, natural mode of communication that helps each of us connect with all life.

Lesson Twelve: Own Your Superpowers

I believe that animal communication can literally save the world. People who not only talk to animals, but listen as well, will have a much harder time contributing to the destruction of the environment. Clear, honest communication builds understanding, and understanding gives birth to compassion. The earth needs more animal communicators. The earth needs more healers. You can be both. I hope you'll do the work required to communicate with animals. You can save the world, one happy ending at a time. All you have to do is keep practicing until you can always *hear them speak.*

Figure 58: *Every animal on this earth has a story to tell and wisdom to share. The lives and futures of humans and animals on this earth are intertwined. Together, we will prosper or perish. Which do you choose? What are you willing to fight for? Are you willing to hear them speak?*

Lesson Twelve: Own Your Superpowers

LESSON TWELVE HIGHLIGHTS

🐾 In this last lesson, we reviewed a few important things you need to remember, and we looked into the many different ways you might decide to use your newfound superpowers to heal the world.

🐾 It doesn't matter whether you choose to keep your abilities private and only use them to forge a deeper connection with our own animal companions, or keep building your abilities until you become the world-renowned animal communicator you are capable of being. Either way, you will make a profound difference in your life and in the lives of everyone you touch.

🐾 It doesn't matter how you decide to use your abilities, as long as you decide that in one way or another, you will contribute to the greater good. Accept your gifts and talents and increase them by your continuing commitment to practice and learn.

🐾 You *can* change the world, one happy ending at a time. All you have to do is claim your ability to *hear them speak*.

🐾 Now...

LESSON TWELVE TASK

I will leave you with just one very important task. Go forth with your new superpowers and save the world!

Lesson Twelve: Own Your Superpowers

Figure 59: *Who's afraid of the big bad wolf? Not me! And not you, either, right? Photo of me and Jake by Therese Clinton.*

Appendix One: More about Meditation

You know by now that animal communication requires a clear mind. And meditation unclutters your mind. When you first begin to meditate, you may have trouble calming your mind. Over time and with practice, it will get easier. After a while, you will be able to go into a deep state of meditation with ease. It will help you in your communication with animals, and it will also assist in your relationships with other humans. It will show you how to be fully present in your mind, your body, and your life.

There are just-about as many ways to meditate as there are people doing it. It really doesn't matter which way you decide to meditate, as long as you commit to quieting your mind for a little while every day. Meditation changes your brain chemistry and your body in positive ways, so even though it may feel like a waste of time, it isn't. Our society is hard-wired to stay busy, and we are socialized to feel that we don't have time to waste just sitting around and staring into space.

But time spent meditating is time well-spent. Eventually, your daily meditation will have the effect of calming your mind even when you are not actively meditating. You'll have less stress, more patience, and a better outlook on life. You'll be healthier in mind, body, and spirit.

One form of meditation may work for you—until it doesn't.

Appendix One: More about Meditation

If that happens, try a new method. Learn to meditate in more than one way so you will be able to do whatever works best on any given day.

Here are some meditation methods I have tried, though you can find many more by searching the internet.

Guided Visual Meditation

If you are new to meditating, this is a super-easy way to get started. An audio recording guides you through a visual meditation. Easy-peasy. Guided meditations are versatile, so try several. (Check out my website, www.HearThemSpeak.com for some of my favorites.)

Meditating can be very relaxing, so staying awake may be a challenge. If you find yourself dozing off, sit in a chair rather than lying down, although some guided meditations are designed for use while falling asleep.

When I listen to my sleeping meditation, I wear comfy headphones that are embedded in a stretchy headband that can double as a sleep mask. (This works great if your sleeping partner snores. Meditation isn't against the law; killing your snoring spouse is.)

Just be careful not to set the same-always audio file to play in a continuous loop. Listening to the same tones repeating for hours at a stretch can make your ears ring (as I figured out for myself). It is best to make a long playlist or have the recording stop after it has played to the end.

Centering Prayer

Centering Prayer involves sitting still and relaxed with your eyes closed. You can sit in a chair—no floor-cushions or fancy yoga positions required. This method is great when you have a few minutes in the car, like waiting for kids in the pick-up lane at school, or sitting in an airport. You can do this just about anywhere, even in public, and nobody knows you are meditating unless you tell them.

Here's how it works:

The first time you do Centering Prayer, as you sit with your eyes closed and your hands relaxed in your lap, you'll decide on a "sacred word." It doesn't have to be anything religious or serious or even very sacred-sounding. Just let your mind float and see what comes up. For years, my sacred word was FREE. I liked it because it meant many things. Freedom from the captivity of a whirling mind, freedom to be myself, freedom to do what I wanted in life. Other sacred words might be LOVE, or SMILE, or RELAX, or REST. It doesn't matter. If you want your sacred word to be CHOCOLATE, that is just fine.

After you have found your sacred word, it can be your sacred word for the rest of your life. Or, another, better word may come to you later.

Appendix One: More about Meditation

Start out doing Centering Prayer for about five minutes a day (unless you're already accomplished at meditating). Use a timer with a soft, non-startling signal. I use my cell phone on silent or vibrate. That way, I'm not tempted to open my eyes and see how much time has passed, and the gentle buzz of the phone's vibration isn't jarring.

With your hands relaxed in your lap and your eyes closed, wait for a thought to cross your mind. When it does, imagine that the thought is a cloud floating across the sky. Without attaching to the thought or coming up with a response to the thought, without judging the thought in any way, you simply watch it float past. Then, wait for the next thought. When it comes, watch it float across your mind until it has disappeared.

At some point, you will find that you have attached to a thought. Instead of watching it float past and disappear, you are thinking about the thought. You have followed it down a rabbit hole; and now, you're obsessing, worrying, planning, figuring, etc. That is when you get to use your sacred word. You don't need to say it out loud (especially if you're in public). Just remember the sacred word, and in doing this, you are blessing and releasing the thought that has temporarily taken over your mind.

At first, you may have to think of your sacred word a gazillion times, because you'll latch on to every little thought that shows up. But over time, you will find that you hardly ever have to use your sacred word, and sometimes you'll even sit there thinking, "I wonder when my next thought will come?" And then you will realize that "I wonder when my next thought will come" was a thought, and then watch it float past. You may be able to work up to several minutes of a quiet, blank mind. It's an incredible feeling.

Shamanic Journeying

Shamanic Journeying is a meditation practice that involves listening to a slow, monotonous drum beat that helps you to reach a deep state of meditation, slowing your heart rate and your mind. To do this form of meditation, you need to take a class from someone who will teach you the process. Shamanic Journeying, in addition to being a great way to meditate, can also be used as a healing modality.

Staring at a Focal Point

Another form of meditation involves staring into a candle flame or some other focal point. The act of staring can help you achieve a light trance state. Think about times when you've daydreamed in class at school by staring out a window. It's a light form of self-hypnosis.

You can also stare at yourself in a mirror. The longer you stare, the more your image will start to blur, and will sometimes morph into strange faces that aren't quite yours. I've seen my image shift so that I resembled an old Indian medicine woman with high

Appendix One: More about Meditation

cheekbones and gray braids. I've also seen my image disappear so completely that I could see the wall behind me. It's a little bit freaky, I guess. So if you're easily freaked-out, maybe save this one for later. (Though I think if you're easily freaked-out, you're probably not reading this.)

Another version of this meditation form is to stare into another person's eyes while they stare into yours—no talking allowed. This can bring up strong emotions, which you and your staring-partner may at first cover by laughing. But the more you stare, the more you build your ability to be fully present in the moment while also being connected to another human being.

Can you see how this would carry over into animal (and human!) communication? You are learning to sit with another person's emotions and your own, without trying to change either, but simply being fully present without judgment.

You can also do this with an animal! Many animals love to meditate with humans. Often, it feels as if they are downloading deep wisdom into your mind while you're staring into each other's souls. Without thought, without words, without agendas.

Meditating with Animals

My most amazing experience with animal-partnered-meditation was with an ocelot named Macho, a resident of the Panther Ridge Conservation Center run by Judy Berens, in

Wellington, Florida. When I was visiting there, I spoke with each of the cats at the center, but I really fell in love with Macho.

Macho had the reputation of being disinterested in most visitors, preferring to lounge up-high in his tree and gaze down from a distance. But for me, Macho sat close to the fence and invited me to stare into his large, expressive eyes. I felt blessed that he chose to connect with me when he spurned others. Though ego has no place in animal communication, I felt proud that Macho had selected me as someone worth knowing.

Macho was clearly an ascended master and an accomplished hypnotist. When I stared into his eyes, all thought fell away, and I was taken immediately into a deep state of meditation. I felt that he was downloading information that couldn't be perceived in words or images.

I have no idea what that information might have been, because it didn't come in words or images. But the connection between Macho and me is something I will never forget. It was more intense than the connection I've felt when communicating telepathically with animals; in fact, when Judy asked questions for me to relay to Macho, I had to "pull back" in order to ask the questions and receive Macho's answers.

Appendix One: More about Meditation

Figure 60: *Macho the elusive hypnotist ocelot. Photo provided by Judy Berens.*

When I communicated with Macho telepathically, the people around me faded from my consciousness as I stepped into the space of communication with Macho. Though we were surrounded by people, we were alone together, sharing a heart-to-heart and mind-to-mind conversation.

But when I stared into Macho's eyes and allowed him to pull me into a mutual meditation, my edges and his blurred together until we became one: One heart, one mind, one being. The telepathic connection between us dissolved, because there is no need to connect that which isn't separate.

To experience this incredible union, you don't have to find a Macho to commune with. Ask any cat or dog or guinea pig or fish if they'd like to meditate with you. If they say yes, you're in for an incredible experience.

Figure 61: *I took this picture at a botanical garden's pond when my husband and I were on vacation with friends in Oregon. Vacations can be wonderful getaways from real life, but in the hectic rush to see and do everything, it's easy to allow time away from home to be just as stressful as the time we spend juggling everyday responsibilities. Like many animal communicators, psychics, and artistic types, I need plenty of alone-time to recharge. To avoid the possibility of getting grumpy and hard-to-live-with, all I had to do was spend a few minutes sitting on the raised walkway above the koi pond, communing with the fish and letting them share with me what it feels like to be supported by the water, taking in oxygen through their gills, swimming and floating lazily with nothing more on the agenda than to swim, to eat, and to simply BE.*

Hug a Tree!

Go out into nature and sit with trees or rocks or water. It's similar to the staring thing, but this time you're not staring, you're watching. You're just observing, being with whatever life forms happen to be there. You're syncing your energy with the energy of nature. This is a good way to align your frequency with the frequency of communication. If you're lucky, you may be able to merge with the spirit of the land the way I merged with Macho's spirit. You may start out by sitting in nature. Then you may progress into sitting with nature. Then, maybe, you'll be granted the miracle of becoming one with nature.

Appendix One: More about Meditation

Figure 62: *These two old granddaddy trees have a lot of wisdom and comfort to share. If the thought of hugging them makes you think of crawling bugs and spiders, just sit near them. Inhale the oxygen-rich air they provide. Take some deep breaths and let the peace and serenity of these ancient and wise counselors seep into your soul.*

Moving Meditation

There are many activities that can help you meditate, even if you have trouble sitting still long enough to get into a meditative state. Moving meditations allow your mind to float, and sometimes as you get into the flow, you reach the quiet-mind state without trying to force it. Here are some examples of moving meditation:

---

walking *running* horseback riding **cycling**

swimming gardening SCULPTING *painting*

drawing cleaning cooking kayaking paddle boarding

dancing *yoga* Tai Chi Qi Gong *singing*

hiking *strumming* **drumming** *stretching*

skateboarding climbing *chanting* *and...*

Appendix One: More about Meditation

Figure 63: *Some days, I meditate with a paintbrush in my hand. This painting illustrates a dream in which I astral-traveled to a strange land where crystal-colored buildings grew up out of the ground; and a wise-woman reminded me to use crystal grids to assist in my clients' healing. The woman's hands display the yogic "gesture of no fear," her left hand cupped to receive, her right hand raised to project, meaning, "I'm not afraid to give; I'm not afraid to receive."*

Appendix Two: Psychic and Emotional Protection

You don't have to do everything (or even anything) that I do. But you do need to do something. At the very least, set an intention that you won't leak or project your own energy, and you won't absorb or invite any energy that isn't yours.

I use quartz crystals that I've charged to keep me safe when I do my work, even if I'm working remotely, sitting in front of my computer connecting with an animal in another location. (To "charge" a crystal for any purpose, hold the crystal in your hand, close your eyes, and communicate your intention to the crystal through your thoughts. It's that simple!)

Before beginning any session, I sit for a moment with both feet flat on the floor, my hands relaxed in my lap, my eyes closed. I take a few quiet breaths, imagining that my breath is flowing down through my feet on the exhale, and up through the top of my head on the inhale.

I imagine that my body is like an empty straw, and my breath is going up and down through that hollow space. I imagine that when I inhale, I am breathing in through the top of my head, through my crown chakra as it opens to admit the peace and wisdom of Source energy.

I imagine that when I exhale, any dense or heavy energy is flowing through the soles of my feet and into the earth, where it will be absorbed and transmuted into something good. As I

Appendix Two: Psychic and Emotional Protection

breathe mindfully in and out for a few breaths, I am cleansing my body, mind, and sprit of anything that doesn't belong.

When I feel that I am clear, I visualize that I am connected to the core of the earth through my base chakra and to the energy of the heavens through my crown chakra. I expand my energy outward into my aura, pushing out anything that doesn't belong, filling my aura with healing white light, and coating it with a translucent pink bubble of protection. Then, with the soles of my feet still rooted to the core of the earth (you can imagine yourself growing roots if that helps) and my mind and spirit connected to Source energy, I silently ask for protection.

Here are some ideas for protection prayers, requests, and intentions that you can mix and match, take or leave. Choose the elements that feel right for you, but be specific. Don't invite just anyone or anything to come on in.

I call on the *(protection / wisdom / guidance / healing / assistance, etc.)* ***of*** *...*

(Source Energy, God, Father Sky, Mother Earth, Guardians of the Earth, the Angelic Realm, the Ascended Masters, Jesus, Archangel Michael, Archangel Raphael, the Guardians and Keepers of the Light, Divine Love, Eternal Light, my Spirit Guides, my Power Animals, my Higher Self, etc.)

I ask; I know that I receive, and I am grateful.

Your religious beliefs may dictate that you only ask God for help. If so, that's fine. Ask God for help. You may be atheist or agnostic and choose not believe that any powers exist outside yourself. That's fine, too. Simply set your intention to be protected from any outside influences, including the emotions of others.

Whether your clearing/grounding/protecting ritual is a prayer, a request, or a reminder for yourself, it's important to set the intention to block any influence or energy that isn't in alignment with your best interests.

Your way doesn't have to be like mine. Develop something that works for you, and use it.

You may also decide to ask the animal's higher self, angels, etc. to assist. Feeling that you have access to a team of helpers can allow you to release your fears and let your intuitive skills emerge.

Appendix Three: Index of Figures

Figure 1: *You've already communicated telepathically with animals many times. But until you learn the difference between receiving true communication and creating something in your imagination, you won't know whether you're communicating or not. Soon, you'll have the tools to enter the space of communication and know when you're there. Animals will be your best teachers! Here are two of mine: Mr. Jack, The Best Good Dog, and Princess Julie-Jules, a Diva who likes to roll in dead things.* ***1***

Figure 2: *In the old, grainy photos that remain of me as a child, it seemed I was almost-always holding a dog or a cat. In this photo: a Pekingese puppy.* ***5***

Figure 3: *While this book will give you the guidance and tools you need to communicate, animals will be your teachers. Ask them to help you, and they will.* ***19***

Figure 4: *Observation can help you tell when an animal is ready to communicate. Animals who are communicating telepathically often look as if they're in a deep trance or about to fall asleep. Notice that Todd the fox isn't looking at me; he is focusing on an inner landscape of memory that he is conveying to me through images, words, and feelings. Some animals will communicate while they're looking at you or even noodling around the room. But when you see this "inner focused" expression, you can be sure the animal is doing its part to connect. Photo by Therese Clinton.* ***21***

Figure 5: *This precious puppy ended up at the animal shelter where I volunteered and practiced my animal communication skills. Even animal companions with perfect pedigrees and exemplary behavior find themselves in shelters; they show up in* need of help, understanding, and the kind of counseling that only animal communicators can give. Some are lost; others simply didn't fit in with the family as expected. Situations change, and people change their minds about what's most important to them. Human companions die or move away. For a multitude of reasons, perfectly good friends-for-life are abandoned, left alone to wonder why they have been discarded. Many animals who are surrendered to shelters have no idea why they weren't allowed to stay with their families. Most would have done anything to stay in the homes they'd thought would be theirs forever. If only they'd understood what was expected of them, things might have been different. Animal communicators are in a unique position to save the world, one forgotten, misunderstood animal at a time.............. **23**

Figure 6: *As an animal communicator, you must be a neutral, empty vessel through which telepathic information can flow. Strong emotion, opinion, or personal agenda can hamper this. Even thinking, Awww, she's so cute! Can keep you from experiencing the depth of wisdom an animal has to offer.*............... **32**

Figure 7: *This is Jack, our three-legged Best Good Dog and Most Benevolent Pack Leader during his tenure here. In this photo, he was in his prime, and the two of us communicated easily. But toward the end of his life, my fear of knowing how much he suffered physically kept me from communicating with him effectively. My emotional attachment made it hard for me to accept the message when he wanted my help to cross the Rainbow Bridge. I didn't want to let him go. Jack was also conflicted; his spirit wanted to stay, but his body was failing. Strong emotions on both our parts made clarity hard to achieve.* **34**

Figure 8: *This is our Solomon Island Eclectus, Ruby. She feels safe in her tidy little cage; too much open space makes her feel exposed and vulnerable. When we tried to move her into a larger cage, she*

Appendix Three: Index of Figures

sat in one corner and squawked until we gave her back the sense of security she needed. Though the other birds enjoy spending time in the outdoor aviary when the weather is nice, Ruby hates it and can't wait to come back inside. **38**

Figure 9: Gregory the goat might have something important to say to Lambert the ram, but Lambert's mind is on something else. If your brain is churning, you'll have a hard time creating a calm, empty mind-space for communication to enter. **42**

Figure 10: In this photo taken by fellow animal communicator Therese Clinton, I'm kissing Sweet Boy, a deer who can't live in the wild because he was captured as a fawn and neutered when his antlers were just beginning to grow. I don't have to wonder if he yearns to be free, because I can converse with him and know that he is happy and well cared for since wildlife conservation authorities brought him to Jungle Exotics sanctuary. To have the opportunity to get this close to animals that aren't ususally domesticated, you have to understand when it is safe and appropriate to interact with an animal, and when it isn't. **49**

Figure 11: This sweet kitty wanted me to come inside her enclosure and pet her. I asked whether she would bite. Her response: "Only if you try to leave." Photo by Therese Clinton. **55**

Figure 12: Asking for protection can be as simple as, well, asking for it. Your prayer or request or intention is yours alone; make it as spare or as elegant as you like. Inked art by Tessa de Jongh..... **58**

Figure 13: I took this photo on our travels in Florida. Pelicans are powerful, but humble. They are much larger than you'd think, and not to be trifled with. (Beware that beak! Mind those wings!) Strong and capable, pelicans don't care what anyone thinks of them. Meek and unassuming, they don't feel diminished when they need to ask for help (or a handout). Pelicans understand that there is strength in humility. They know their potential, they are open to possibilities, and they accept their limitations. Be a pelican. **65**

Figure 14: When I communicated with Zuma, he showed an image of himself rolling in hay, and another of getting his mane brushed. He was jealous of a special needs lion who got more attention (and hay, and hair-brushing) than he did. Not understanding the reason the other lion got so much coddling, he claimed, "I can do anything better than him! He's not as great as he thinks he is!" A couple of days after I left the sanctuary, Zuma was granted both of his wishes. My friend sent videos of him playing in a pile of hay then getting his mane brushed. It was so gratifying to see the expression of bliss on his face! It takes such simple things to make an animal happy. Photo by Therese Clinton. **73**

Figure 15: A small dog, afraid of being stepped-on, may show an image of the only thing she can see clearly from her viewpoint. There won't be faces, or any part of the humans other than a towering forest of legs and larger-than-life feet that she has to avoid. **81**

Figure 16: It is easy to observe from this photo that Charlie the cheetah feels bad. When I asked, "Hey, Bud, what's wrong?" Charlie showed me an image of a green beach ball swelling in his belly. Had Charlie somehow swallowed a beach ball? No, of course not. But he felt bloated, and green is the universal color for nausea. Charlie couldn't tell me (because he didn't know) what had caused his discomfort. But knowing what the problem was, Charlie's caregivers at Panther Ridge were able to treat Charlie's intestinal upset and then do some detective work to find out which food had caused the problem. Photo by Anne-Laure Michelis. **84**

Appendix Three: Index of Figures

Figure 17: *Even a rattlesnake can be as eloquent as any poet: "I have lived near your house and watched you from a distance, keeping a respectful space so as not to cause you fear. I am both humble and powerful. I have great love for all things. I am not violent or cruel. I help animals who are ready to transform into spirit, striking quickly and accurately so they don't suffer. I assist them with love and reverence for their life and spirit, and I experience their transformation along with them. Their bodies as food are a gift back to me for my loving help with their transformation."* **91**

Figure 18: *Felicia's personality and attitude came through clearly with auditory communication. A voice can also come through with a distinct accent or way of thinking. When an animal communicates with a particular accent or personality, you know you're on target. Photo by Celia Lambert.* **93**

Figure 19: *Hazel's prim-and-proper way of speaking reflected her personality. A school teacher at heart, she felt obligated to tutor the other dogs in the family in "proper comportment." Photo by Celia Lambert.* **95**

Figure 20: *Tango, the poo-eating guru, AKA Poo-ru* **103**

Figure 21: *Our cat Max feels more like a dog than a cat. His consciousness state is that of a big dog. Large and in-charge, he trains puppies to respect cats. If he likes being a dog so much, why is he a cat? Because cats are able and allowed to do things that dogs can't, including lying on top of the papers on my desk when I'm trying to work....* **111**

Figure 22: *Our cat Ulrich (Ulrich von Lickshimself) has a hitch in his get-along. His hips are off-kilter from an old injury. Connect with Ulrich telepathically and see whether your attention wants to* stick in one particular area of his spine. Is one area hazy, dark, or shaded in your mind's eye when you look at this picture and ask to see where it hurts? **119**

Figure 23: This is our cat, Princess Grace. A good question to ask a cat is "Can you show me what it feels like to purr?" **122**

Figure 24: I was connected telepathically to Ella at the moment she crossed the Rainbow Bridge. A wash of cold air swept through my body when she transcended her physical form and became pure spirit. Photo by Michael Loftis. **125**

Figure 25: If you asked Jed to tell you about his favorite place, he might send you a memory of the taste of salt water and the smell of ocean air. Here he is, passed out on the Sharknado towel after a long day of chasing balls on the beach. **141**

Figure 26: This stray dog had a hard time trusting people enough to get in the car with someone who wanted to help her. Animal communication and energy healing gave her the courage to allow herself to be rescued. Photo by Lauren Thomas. **147**

Figure 27: Bella, before animal communication helped her wishes to be understood. Photo by Anne-Laure Michelis. **152**

Figure 28: Bella, enjoying her excursion into a different enclosure after she was able to tell us what she wanted. See how happy and relaxed she looks? Photo by Anne-Laure Michelis. **155**

Figure 29: Esmeralda is a good communicator, but if you're blocked, you won't understand what she wants you to know. **161**

Figure 30: Fear of what I might learn kept me from even asking my missing goats and Lambert where they were. A foolish decision

Appendix Three: Index of Figures

I soon came to regret. In the future, I'll try not to allow fear to keep me from even trying to communicate in an emotionally-charged situation. **166**

Figure 31: People (and animals) often have strong opinions about how things should be. Should dogs sleep in the house? Jed thinks not. He wants to be outside patrolling all night long. But he isn't in charge around here, so he has to sleep inside. If you have an opinion about how animals should live, set it aside when you're communicating. **177**

Figure 32: Our dog Bear was ruled by his hormones. Even after he was neutered, he managed to "hook up" with a female dog in estrus. I called the vet in a panic, but he assured me that Bear was shooting blanks. **183**

Figure 33: Notice that Zuma isn't looking at me, though it is clear that he is connected-in telepathically. Animals who are communicating will often stare into space instead of looking at you. Photo by Therese Clinton.. **189**

Figure 34: Notice Zuma's faraway expression. Animals who are communicating often get a faraway look in their eyes and an expression of going-inward on their faces. Photo by Therese Clinton. **190**

Figure 35: Tomo paced along the edges of his enclosure while communicating, but he still had that same faraway look on his face. Photo by Therese Clinton... **191**

Figure 36: Sometimes the animal will look directly at you while communicating, and it will be obvious from their expression that they are paying attention to you. Photo by Therese Clinton. **192**

Figure 37: Animals who are experiencing a shift during energy healing will often yawn. Photos by Therese Clinton. **193**

Figure 38: Your own animal companions are happy to help you practice your animal communication skills and move past any blocks you have. But if you need more animal helpers, consider visiting your local animal shelter. You can do a lot of good there, even without bringing home new family members. **199**

Figure 39: Good advice from Zen Kitty Princess Grace: Take the time to care for yourself, and rest when you need to. You can't be a clear channel if you're tired. **206**

Figure 40: When Gabrielle met Opus during an animal communication class at Dragonfly Pond Farm, Opus communicated, "I want to go home with you!" Gabrielle was reluctant to tell me, but I already knew Opus wanted a little adventure. It would have been a terrible shame if Gabrielle had blocked—or talked herself out of—the communication she received. You will be asked to broach potentially delicate subjects. Be mindful how you deliver sensitive information, but don't hold back when an animal asks you to tell their human companion something important. **208**

Figure 41: It can be hard to communicate with our own animals, especially when we worry they might tell us something we don't want to hear. When Jack started feeling bad, it was easy to tell through simple observations. What he wanted us to do for him (and when) was harder to hear, because my emotions were involved. **211**

Figure 42: Jack looking through the window when he was in too much pain to play outside. **214**

Appendix Three: Index of Figures

Figure 43: *This belligerent rooster may not want to communicate with you. That's okay. Every animal you see doesn't have to be your new best friend because you're an animal communicator...* ***220***

Figure 44: *How many dogs in this picture? (Hint: It's not two.) Just another blended family with more animals than people. What could possibly go wrong?* ***229***

Figure 45: *This stray puppy is being trained by our cat Max. He learned to love cats but was a determined chicken-killer; his way of showing us that he would make a better city dog. Every home an animal lands in isn't supposed to be theirs forever. You may have to counsel families on finding the right fit for an animal who wants to live somewhere other than where they are.* ***230***

Figure 46: *Our dog Molly was ready to cross the Rainbow Bridge long before I was ready to let her go. Even though she told me her wishes many times, she still had "good days" that made me hesitate. I had to wait until I was absolutely sure that neither of us would change our mind at the last minute.* ***245***

Figure 47: *Here at Dragonfly Pond Farm, everyone has to get along with everyone else. With more than a dozen species living together, respect for all other family members (and visitors!) is a must. It's the rule, and because of animal communication, everybody knows it. In this photo, Jack and Lightning are in the foreground, with Alyss in the background.* ***251***

Figure 48: *Truman is our special needs dog. He is deaf, has impaired eyesight, and suffers from post-traumatic stress. His right eye is black because the iris is prolapsed, probably due to abuse he suffered as a puppy. I suspect that he also has some brain damage for the same reason. Animal communication and* energy healing saved his life, but he will never be a "normal" dog. Photo by Peter Berry. ***254***

Figure 49: This isn't Rex, but it is a shelter dog, who may have arrived at the shelter with misconceptions that can be uncovered and released with animal communication. ***263***

Figure 50: This little black hen was attacked by a hawk when she was out foraging. I thought she was dead, and so did she, but it turned out that she wasn't... ***275***

Figure 51: You may not believe in ghosts, but Georgia does. I don't have the ability to see ghosts, but Georgia does. Once, when I saw her growling at something in the forest behind our house, I asked what she was looking at. She showed me a group of gray, tattered-looking men in civil-war uniforms, trudging through the forest. I called a friend who is adept at mediumship. She validated Georgia's visions and made a house call to help the lost soldiers find their way to the light. ***278***

Figure 52: Small creatures are easily overlooked if you're not paying attention, but they can provide a valuable viewpoint if you take the time to notice them and listen to the wisdom they have to share. ***289***

Figure 53: Energy healing can, among other things, help animals get along in a multi-species household. These are three of our twelve cats; left-right: Teddy, Max, and Blue. (Yes, I know twelve is a lot, but we have eight acres, plenty of room for all the critters and humans to spread out.) Everyone gets along with everyone else here, because that's the rule, and everybody knows it. ***292***

Appendix Three: Index of Figures

Figure 54: *Volunteering at your local animal shelter can help you hone your skills. And while you are practicing, you have the opportunity to improve the life of every animal you meet.* ***299***

Figure 55: *This is Astrid, whose sense of guilt kept her from bonding with her new family. Now, Astrid has a happy life and a deep bond with her people – human, canine and feline! Photo by Daike Klement.* ***302***

Figure 56: *Boots had a droopy ear, and he felt bad. Both conditions are easy to see from this photo (look at his eyes; he is in pain). But anyone who combined these two separate observations to equal one conclusion would be wrong. And jumping to an erroneous conclusion from a simple observation (or an observation-tainted communication) would deprive Boots and his loving human companion of the opportunity to discover the real problem. Photo by Kevin Wattier.* ***309***

Figure 57: *This young, beautiful, perfectly healthy shelter dog was tired of life, tired of being disappointed by the people she had been foolish enough to trust. She was done, finished; ready to leave this life and start over again. She reminded me so much of a dog I had known and loved, though they looked nothing alike. I promised her that I would adopt her as soon as I returned from a week-long writing retreat. I promised I would come and get her, and I tried to connect with her telepathically every day, but I kept seeing an image of her looking away from me, gazing over a distant horizon. She wasn't at all interested in trusting anyone again, ever. Still, I called the shelter and told them to save her for me. I told them when I would pick her up. But before that could happen, she—this completely gentle spirit—got into a fight with a bigger dog. She was euthanized the day before I was scheduled to bring her home.* ***313***

Figure 58: *Every animal on this earth has a story to tell and wisdom to share. The lives and futures of humans and animals on this earth are intertwined. Together, we will prosper or perish. Which do you choose? What are you willing to fight for? Are you willing to hear them speak?* ***316***

Figure 59: *Who's afraid of the big bad wolf? Not me! And not you, either, right? Photo of me and Jake by Therese Clinton.* ***319***

Figure 60: *Macho the elusive hypnotist ocelot. Photo provided by Judy Berens.* ***327***

Figure 61: *I took this picture at a botanical garden's pond when my husband and I were on vacation with friends in Oregon. Vacations can be wonderful getaways from real life, but in the hectic rush to see and do everything, it's easy to allow time away from home to be just as stressful as the time we spend juggling everyday responsibilities. Like many animal communicators, psychics, and artistic types, I need plenty of alone-time to recharge. To avoid the possibility of getting grumpy and hard-to-live-with, all I had to do was spend a few minutes sitting on the raised walkway above the koi pond, communing with the fish and letting them share with me what it feels like to be supported by the water, taking in oxygen through their gills, swimming and floating lazily with nothing more on the agenda than to swim, to eat, and to simply BE.* ***329***

Figure 62: *These two old granddaddy trees have a lot of wisdom and comfort to share. If the thought of hugging them makes you think of crawling bugs and spiders, just sit near them. Inhale the oxygen-rich air they provide. Take some deep breaths and let the peace and serenity of these ancient and wise counselors seep into your soul.* ***331***

Appendix Three: Index of Figures

Figure 63: *Some days, I meditate with a paintbrush in my hand. This painting illustrates a dream in which I astral-traveled to a strange land where crystal-colored buildings grew up out of the ground; and a wise-woman reminded me to use crystal grids to assist in my clients' healing. The woman's hands display the yogic "gesture of no fear," her left hand cupped to receive, her right hand raised to project, meaning, "I'm not afraid to give; I'm not afraid to receive."* ***333***

Appendix Four: Resources

I have read many books about animal communication and energy healing, and I've taken many courses to learn more. I have learned by teaching and mentoring my students, and I have learned from writing this book, because it made me think deeply and consider all angles so I could break down the information and organize it in a way that would be accessible. I'm always learning, and I hope you'll continue to increase your skills for as long as you live.

Because available resources (books, classes, podcasts, and more) are always changing and expanding, rather than list them here, where the information may one day become obsolete, I keep a list of relevant resources on my website.

Another way to stay in the loop and keep learning more is to keep in touch with me via my newsletter and social media pages. You'll find links to everything in my universe on my website, so I hope you'll visit soon:

www.HearThemSpeak.com

www.ingramcontent.com/pod-product-compliance
Lightning Source LLC
LaVergne TN
LVHW020426070526
838199LV00004B/304